IBM Tivoli Netcool Configuration Manager Proof of Concept Guide

NMS Guru, Inc:
Daniel L. Needles

Saturday, May 11, 2013

Modification History

AUTHOR	DATE	COMMENTS
Daniel L. Needles	10/31/2011	Initial draft.
Daniel L. Needles	5/10/2013	Revamped for publication.

ISBN-10: 0984972250

ISBN-13: 978-0-9849722-5-8

Table of Contents

Executive Summary

Introduction

IBM Tivoli Netcool Configuration Manager (ITNCM) is a later acquisition into the Tivoli Netcool suite. While most of the software within this suite came from Micromuse in 2005, ITNCM was the flag ship of Intelliden, a completely unrelated product with its own conventions and integrations. IBM has always been good at provide volumes of information about the product in the Tivoli suite but less successful at providing simple step by step guides. The purpose of this book is to provide a simple, step by step, implementation of ITNCM for a Proof of Concept. The book walks the reader through a real life, two week long, end-to-end example of a ITNCM POC deployment.

Intelliden provides Configuration and Change management as defined by the FCAPS and ITILv3 standards respectively. Intelliden conforms to the majority of products within this niche which include: HP OpsWare and Versata Alterpoint. It provides for network devices:

- Backup and restoration
- Authentication choke point
- Authorization workflow (code review, management approval of changes, etc.)
- Configuration Governance
    - Automated mass changes
    - Change control and change management
    - Standard deviation detection
    - Automated Standard Enforcement

Overall ITNCM is a very mature solution within this genera of products and able to accommodate a company's primary needs which include:

- Centralized authentication and authorization
- Audit compliance

Like any Network Management Systems (NMS) product the ITNCM is only 15% of the end-to-end solution. The other 85% relies on organizational structure, business processes, knowledge management and probably most important executive sponsorship. As such, the solution is expected to evolve as it is adapted to the organization and automates many of the manual processes and absorbs knowledge management for the organization. However, in the case of a proof of concept these hooks are not as important as the focus is on the implementation of the tool architecture with the purpose of learning the tool set.

What about the Book Cover?

Where ITNCM and other Configuration Manager products differ with the rest of NMS. Unlike any of the other 15 disciplines that could loosely be considered among the niches of the NMS field, configuration management is not passive. Where Fault and Performance management tries to listen and adapt to the network, Configuration management is about reducing variance by enforcing standards and actually eliminate the faults and performance issues to begin with. This is where the cover of this book comes into play. It portrays the 300 Greek standing against the Babylonian hoard. By careful selection of location along with standard practices and procedures, 300 Greeks held off a million men for an extended period of time.

With every strength there is a weakness. The two sides of this coin are wrapped up in that everyone looks and acts the same. There are no heroes. This is what typifies an environment great Configuration Management. Heroes are not a good thing for the overall good. They cannot exist in a fully functioning environment because there is no room to standout. This image of the 300 also indicates its weakness. Strong discipline begets dependence on that discipline. And the lack of the ability to be a hero steers those personalities away from the organization that prevents this sort of creativity. That is, if someone drops their phalanx, the most common response is - "not my job." That is because without room to grow heroes, people get weak on stepping up when it is required.

What this Book Covers

That said, this book is not a strategy book or an in depth discussion of every nook and cranny of ITNCM. This book covers the steps required to install and configure the end-to-end ITNCM tool solution. It does not currently cover the organizational structure and most of the business processes that accompany the tool. This gap is primarily due to the early stage of adoption where these structures and processes are not completely defined. However, it is recommended to add these aspect to the document at a later date.

Summary

This living document is meant to evolve as the ITNCM installation is expected to grow in scope and role. In particular configuration management is a more proactive approach as it reduced the variance among configurations and improves audit controls which both reduce the occurrence of issues and improve the visibility and identification of issues. If done correctly, the ROI of the solution can easily exceed fivefold the expense of the solution.

Prepare System

Introduction

Once the prerequisites have been satisfied, the VM slices created, and the base operating system installed, next the system has to be prepared. This section walks the reader through general system work and ITNCM specific work.

General system work

ITNCM can be installed on a number of platforms. For the purposes of this POC outlined in the book, Redhat/CentOS 5.X was used. The first step is to do a general update of the Redhat/CentOS 5.x system to the latest and greatest packages.

(NOTE: 5.x is installed instead of 6.x due to larger number of issues seen in Redhat/CentOS 6.x installations.)

This procedure will update to latest release of Redhat/CentOS 5.x. The first step is to clean All Packages with the following command:

```
yum clean all
```

The following command will get a list of packages that are going to be updated:

```
yum list updates
```

Next, perform an update

```
yum update
```

Finally reboot the server for Kernel changes to take effect

```
reboot
```

Verify that the version of RedHat or CentOS is the latest and greatest (i.e. CentOS 5.7 in this lab system case):

```
cat /etc/redhat-release

    CentOS release 5.7 (Final)
```

Most likely the packages are up to date if the previous series of commands were entered. The following list of commands will verify:

```
yum install libaio
yum install compat-libstdc++-33
yum install libstdc++
yum install glibc
yum install libgcc
```

NOTE: Because Tivoli Common Reporting installs 32-bit binaries, you must install the 32-bit versions of the prerequisite libraries, even on 64-bit system. Otherwise, the installation will fail. The following system libraries need to be installed:

```
#yum install compat-libstdc++-33 # -33.3.2.3   Already installed above
#yum install compat-glibc        #-2.3.4-2.26  Already installed above
yum install openmotif22          #-2.2.3-18
```

Correct the /etc/hosts file in the following steps. First identify the IP address for the main interface (i.e. eth0)

```
ifconfig -a
```

Then edit the host file:

```
vi /etc/hosts
```

The result should look akin to:

```
   127.0.0.1      localhost
   <IP>      <HOST> <HOST FULL QUALIFIED>
```

The last general system check/fix is to verify that locale is en_US.UTF-8 by entering the following command:

```
locale
```

The result should have all setting to: en_US.UTF-8.

ITNCM Specific Work

ITNCM does not create system users and groups. So do this manually and create and assign the product directory. This is done through the following commands:

```
groupadd icosgrp
useradd -g icosgrp -s /bin/bash -p PASSWORD -m icosftp
useradd -g icosgrp -s /bin/bash -p PASSWORD -m icosuser
## NOTE: Even if FTP is not used you MUST have this chmod statement
##       as "scripts" will log to the directory and without access
##       any change scripts will fail.
chmod 774 /home/icosftp
mkdir -p /opt/IBM/tivoli/netcool/ncm
chown icosuser:icosgrp /opt/IBM/tivoli/netcool/ncm
```

Summary

Once this section is complete the major system configuration will be done.

Uninstall [Optional]

Introduction

If this is a reinstallation, then DB2 and ITNCM + TCR will need to be cleaned out. This section describes the steps required to perform these actions.

DB2 Uninstall

If this is a reinstallation and DB2 needs to be reinstalled, the following steps clean db2 from the system:

```
cd DB2/wser
db2_deinstall -r /root/db2wse.rsp
cd /var
rm -rf db2
cat /etc/group
groupdel db2iadm1
groupdel db2fadm1
groupdel dasadm1
ps -ef | grep -I db2 | awk '{ print $2 }' | xargs kill -9
cd /var;
rm -rf db2
```

ITNCM Uninstall

ITNCM requires several steps to uninstall the software:

```
userdel -r icosftp
userdel -r icosuser
groupdel icosgrp
cd /opt;
rm -rf ibm
cd /tmp;
rm -rf *
cd
rm *log*
ps -ef | grep -I ibm | awk '{ print $2 }' | xargs kill -9
reboot
```

Summary

Once the steps in this section are complete, the software will be uninstalled.

Install DB2

Introduction

After the system has been prepared and any pre-installation of DB2 and ITNCM has been removed, the next step is to install DB2.

Start the GUI

The following commands install DB2

```
cd DB/wser
./db2setup
```

The screen will read:

```
DBI1190I db2setup is preparing the ...
```

GUI Install

After several seconds/minutes a GUI will appear:

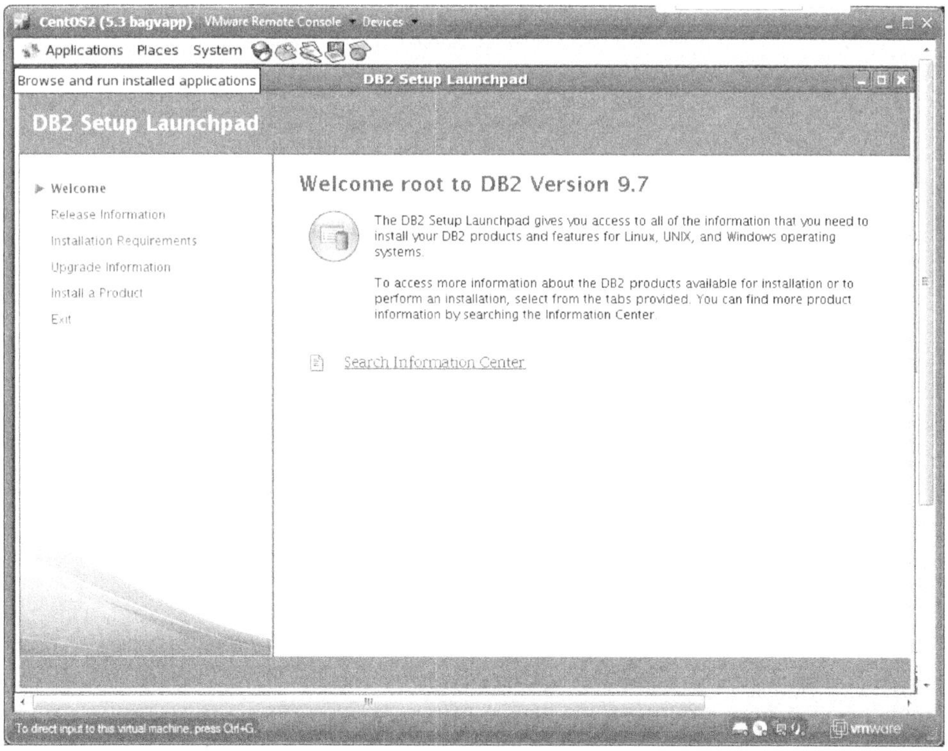

Select Install Product in left menu

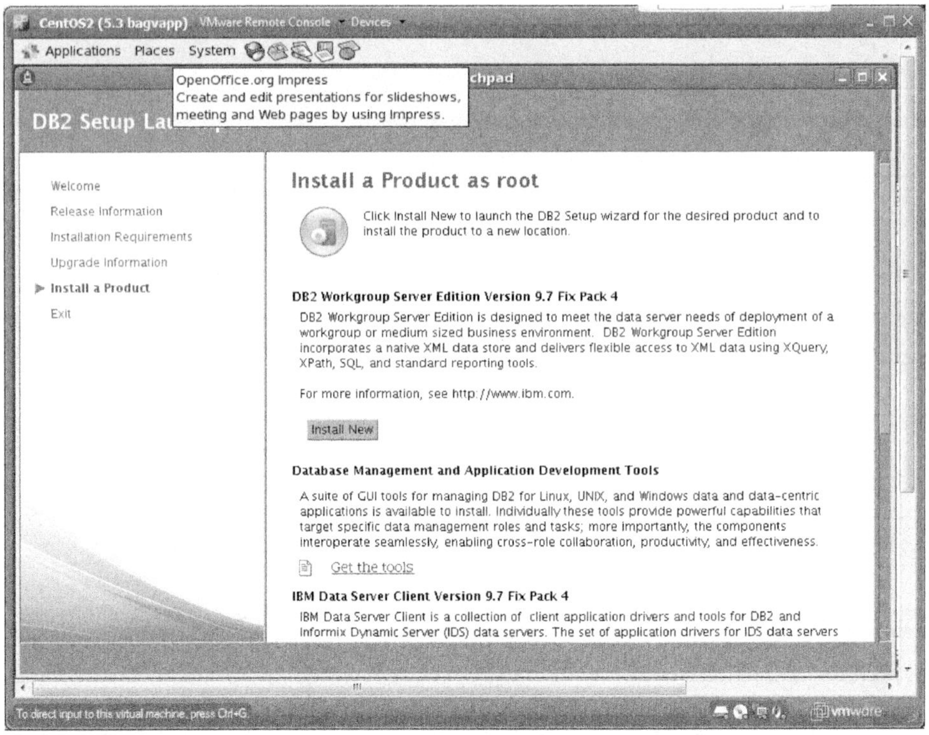

Click first "Install New" button.

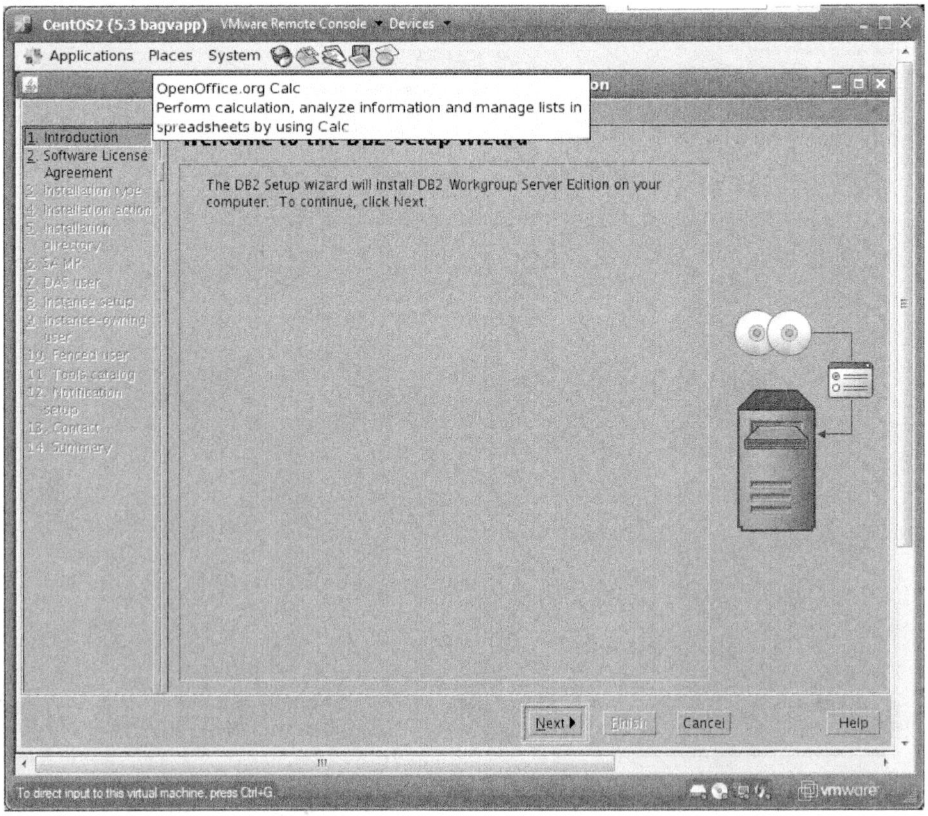

Click Next

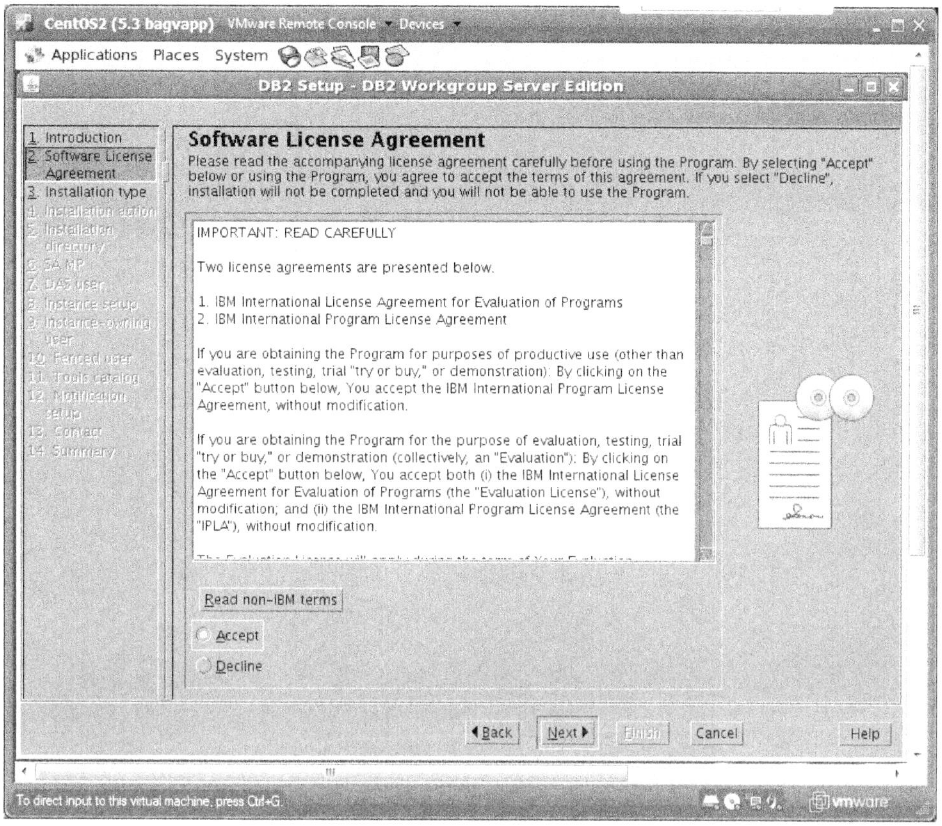

Click Accept radio button and click Next

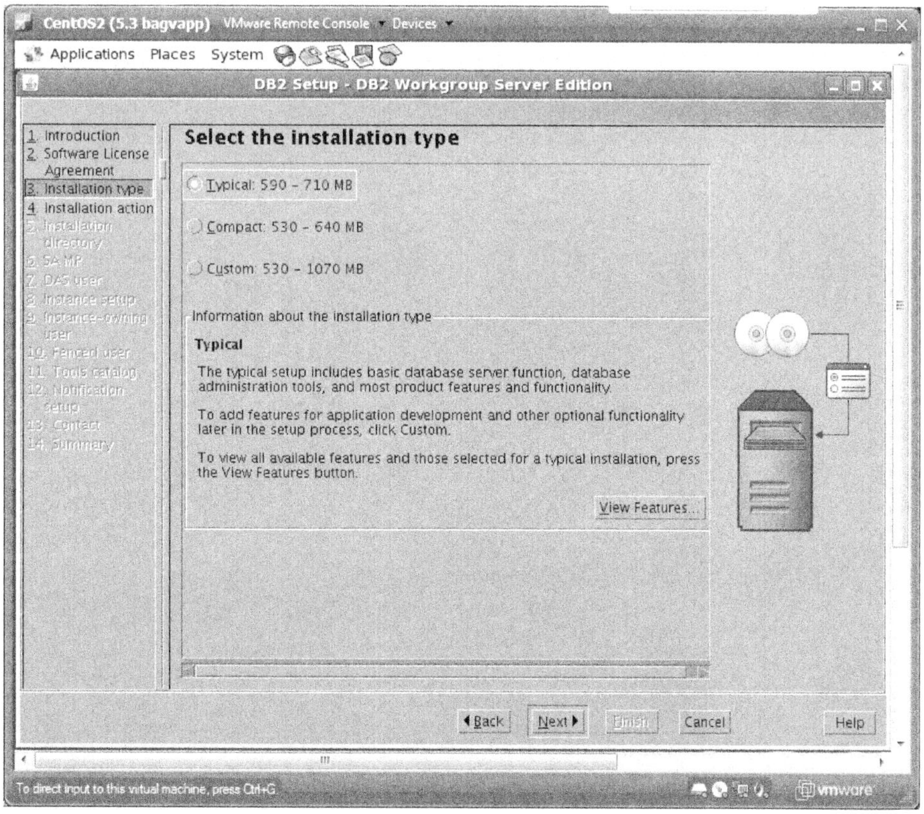

Accept defaults and Click Next button.

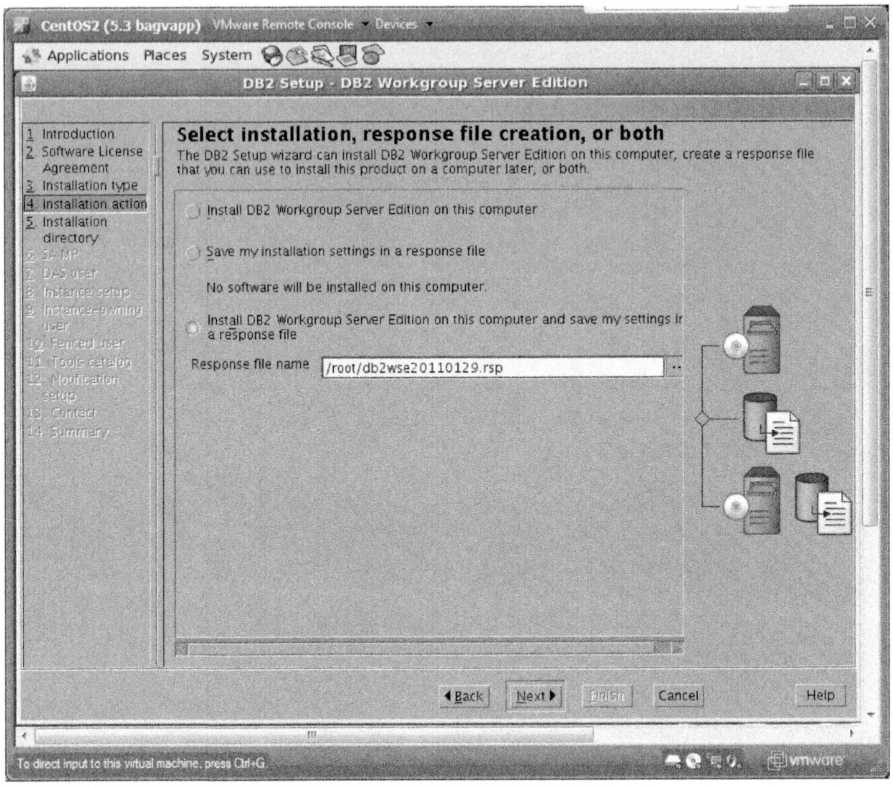

Change file name to include date and click next.

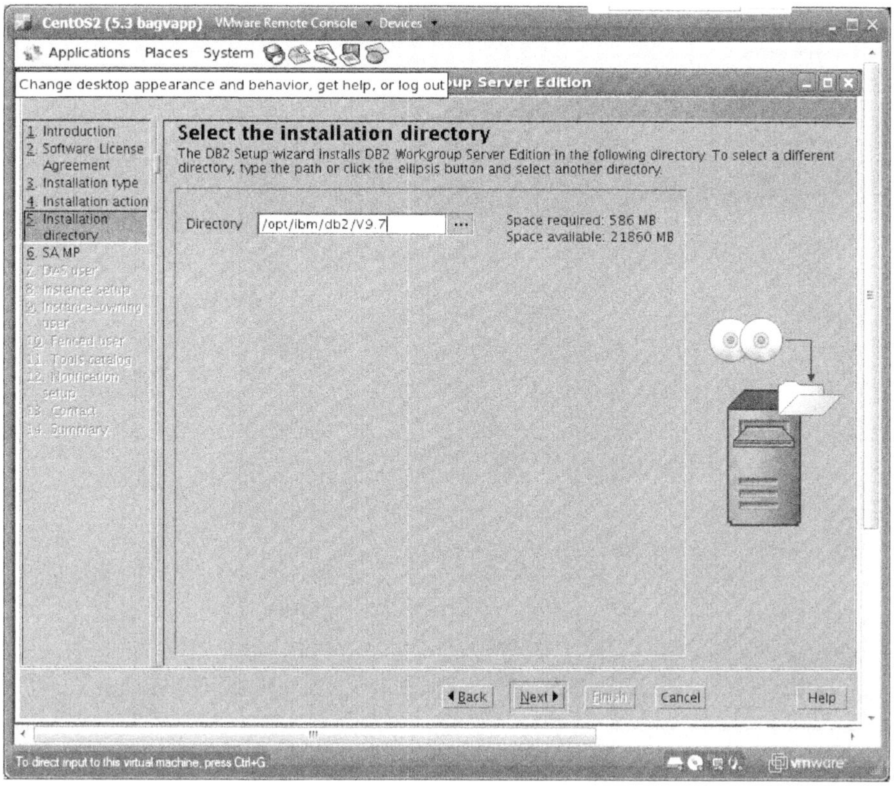

Accept default and click next.

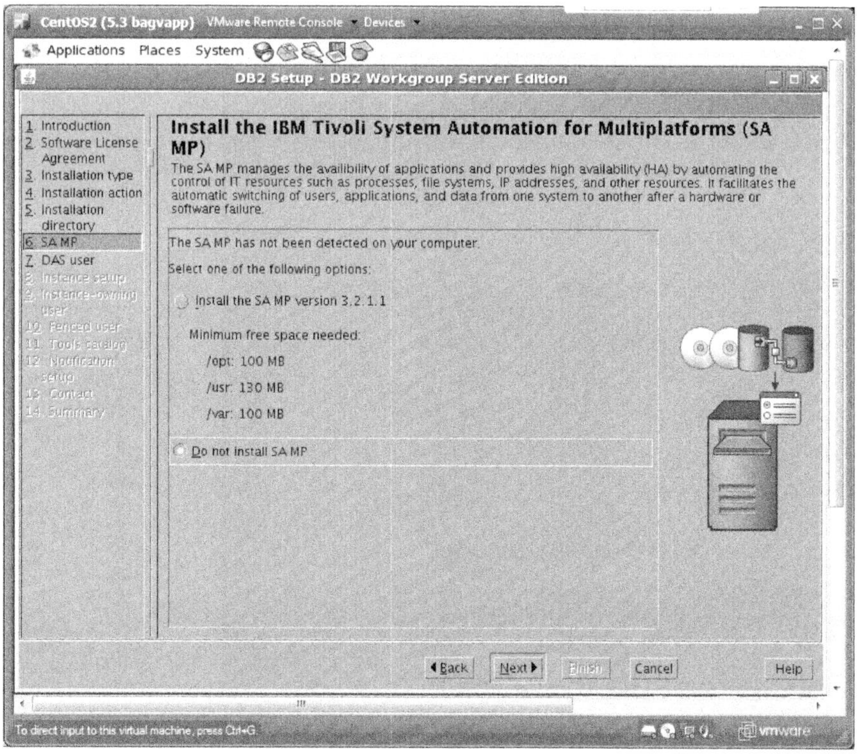

Select to NOT install SA MP and click Next

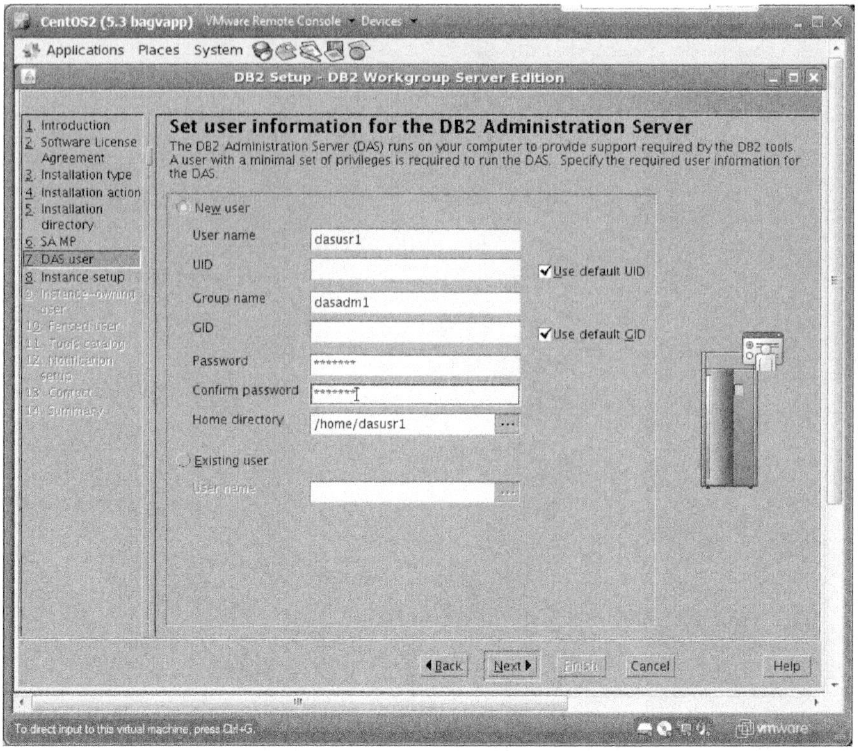

Set password to "PASSWORD" with a 3 for e and zero for o. Accept other defaults and click next.

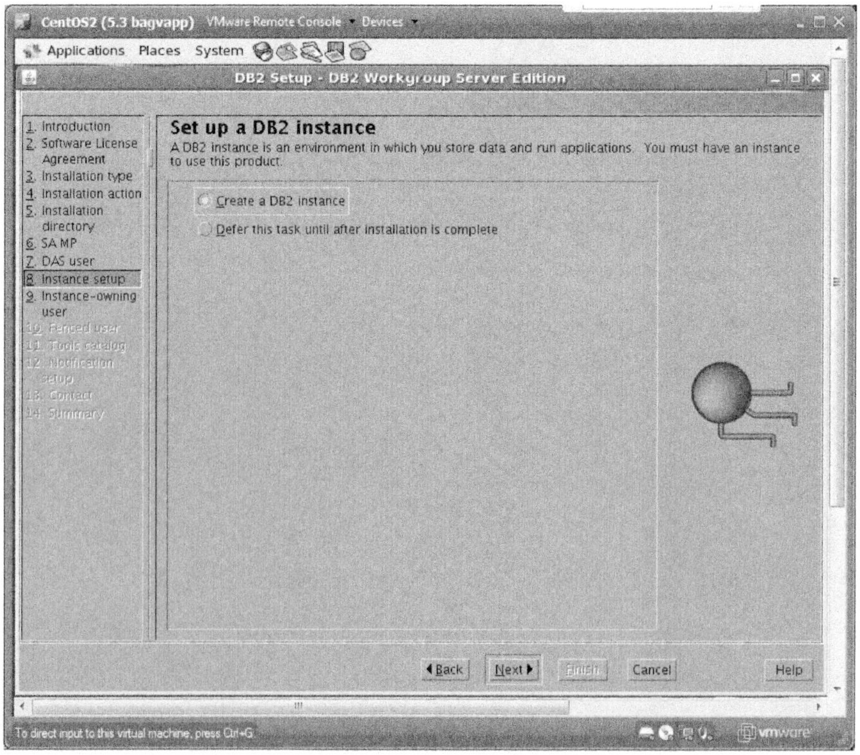

Accept defaults and click next.

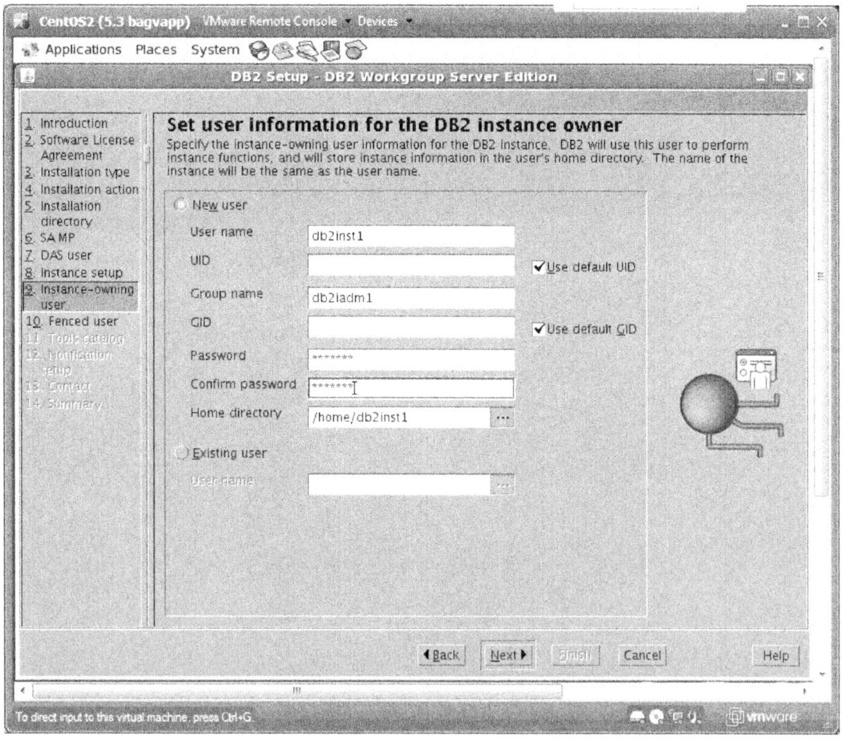

NOTE: If the GUI defaults to db2inst2 that means that /var/db/global.reg was not deleted. Abort the installation and redo the clean up procedure. Set password to same as above (PASSWORD) and click next

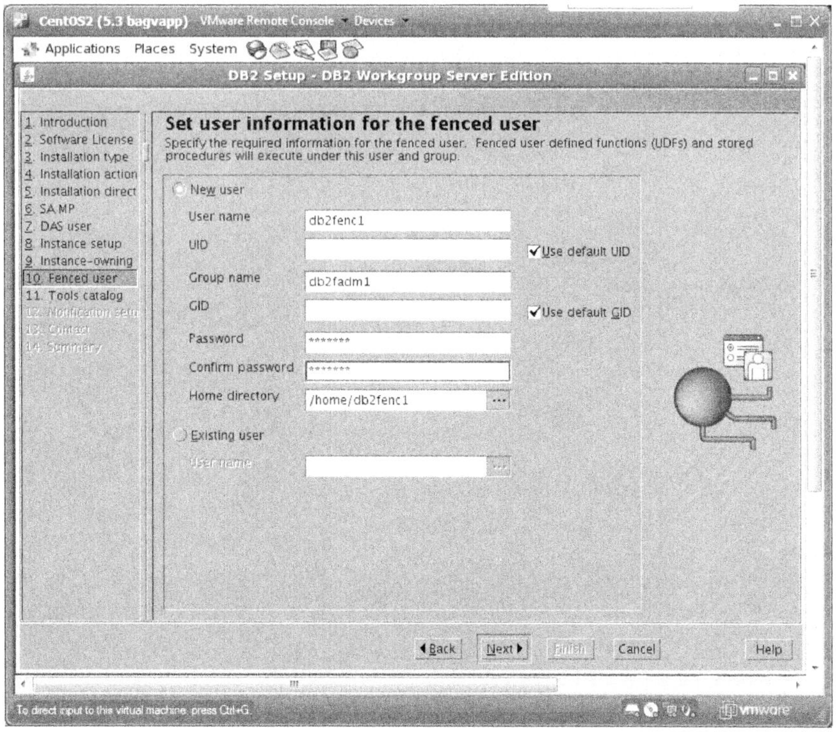

Set password and click next.

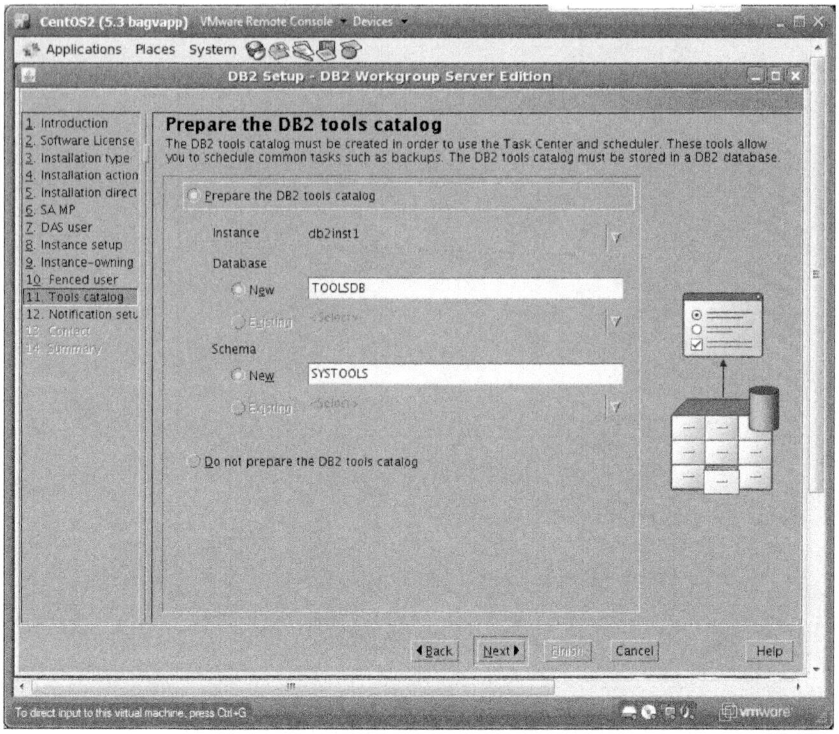

Click to Prepare the DB2 tools catalog and accept the other defaults and click next

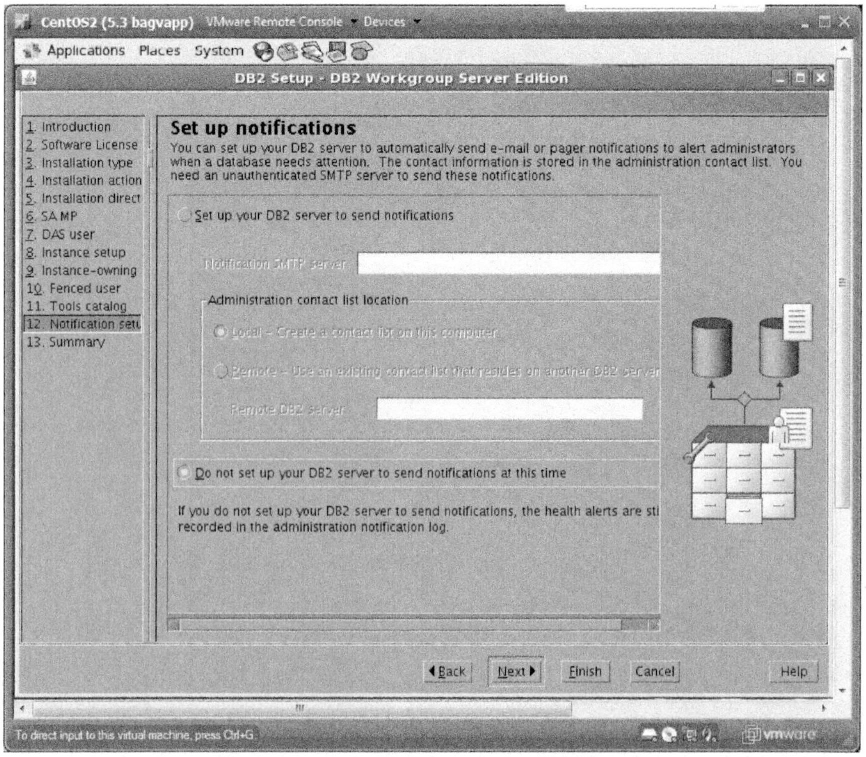

Select to NOT set up notification and click next

This will result in the following screen :

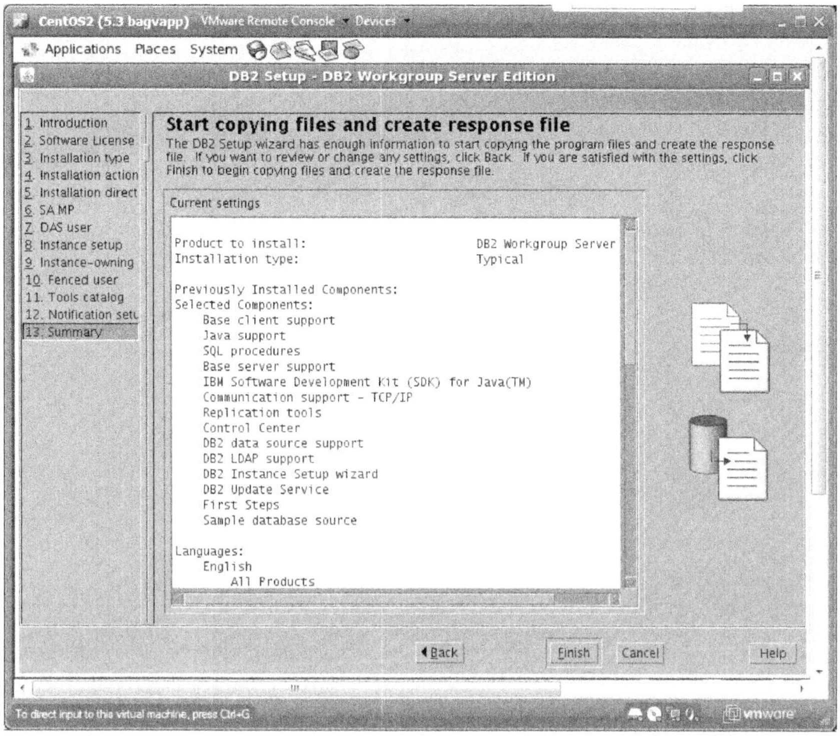

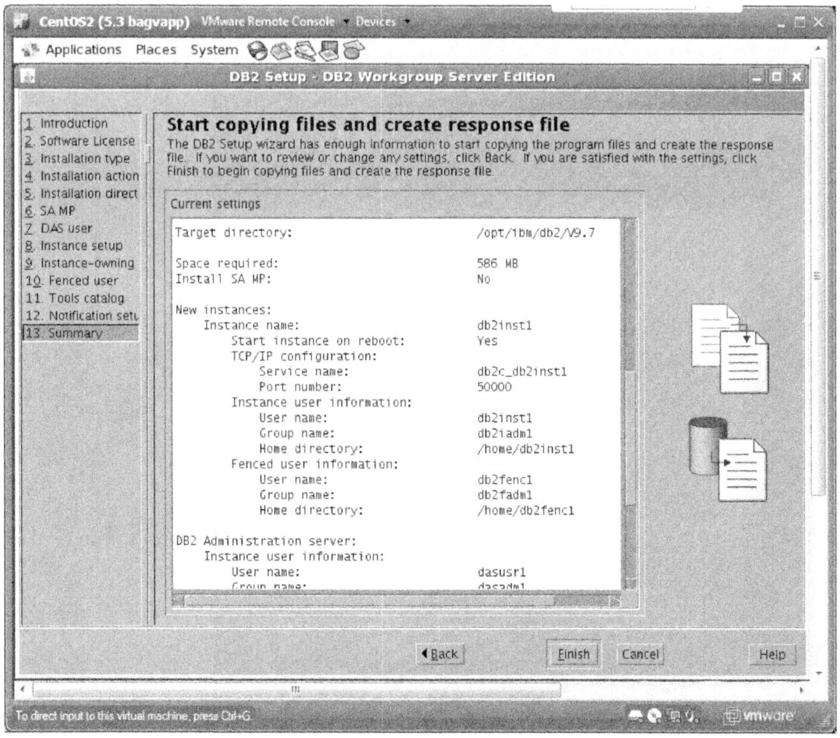

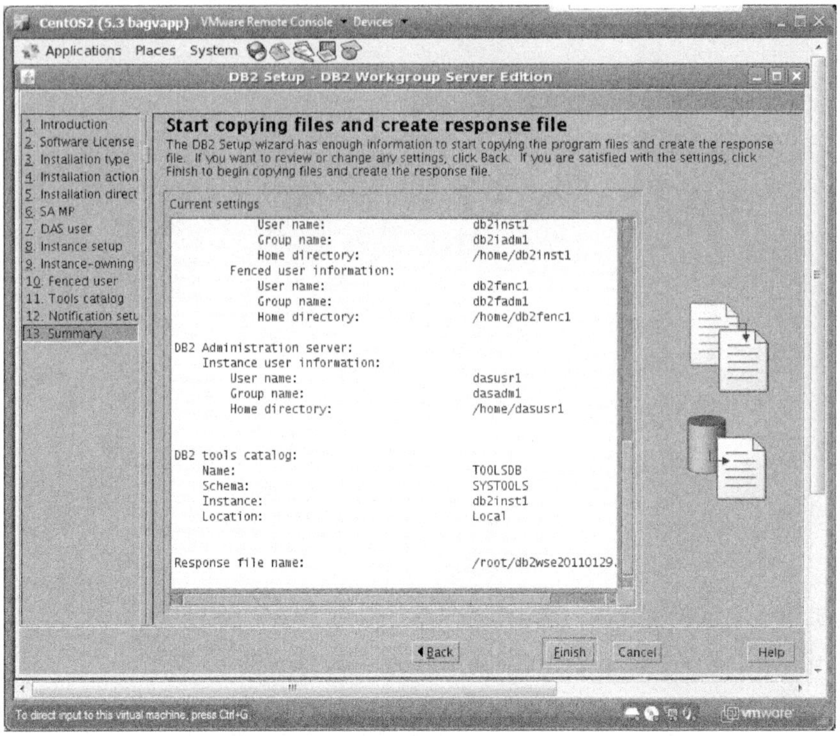

Scroll down and review output. Click Finished

The window will disappear, text be returned to the prompt, and finally an installation window will pop up as follows:

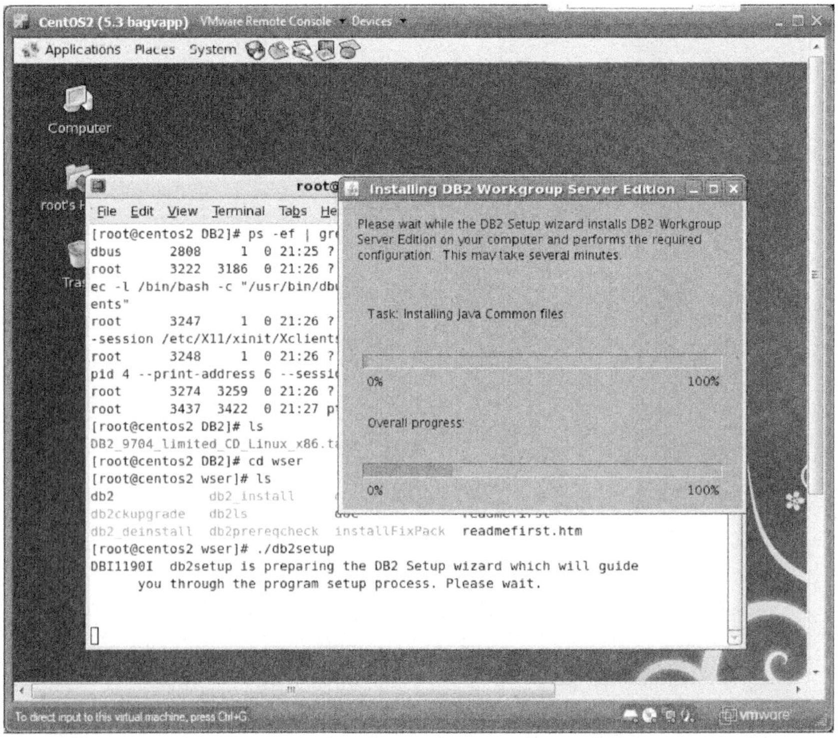

Once complete the following screen will appear. Scroll through the results and verify they are correct.

CentOS2 (5.3 bagvapp)
Applications Places System
Setup Complete
Setup has completed successfully
If you have not already done so, it is recommended that you complete the post-install steps after installation.
You can also review the log file for more details of the setup process. The setup log files db2setup.log and db2setup.err are located in the /tmp directory.
Post-install steps
Log file
Click Finish to exit.
Finish
To direct input to this virtual machine, press Ctrl+G.

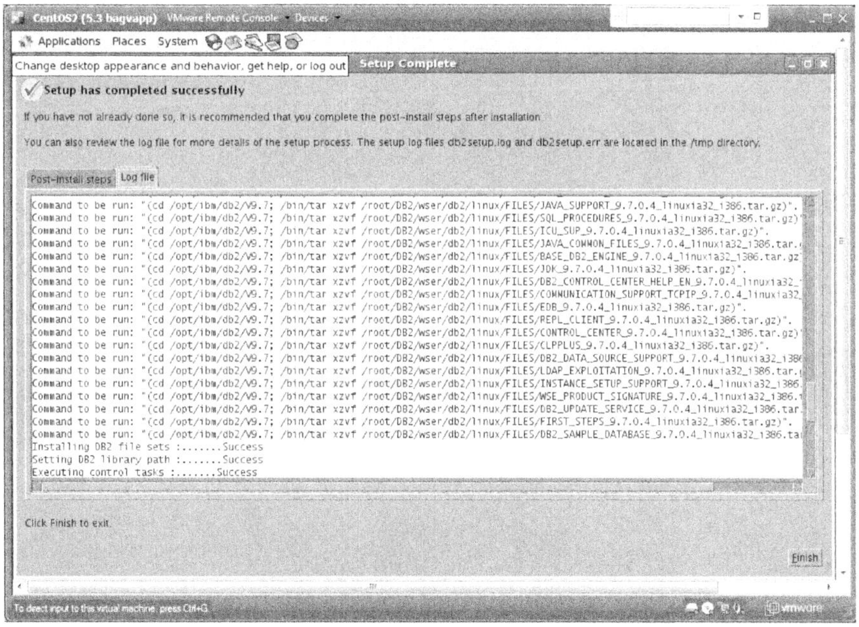
CentOS2 (5.3 bagvapp)
Applications Places System
Change desktop appearance and behavior, get help, or log out
Setup Complete
Setup has completed successfully
If you have not already done so, it is recommended that you complete the post-install steps after installation.
You can also review the log file for more details of the setup process. The setup log files db2setup.log and db2setup.err are located in the /tmp directory.
Post-install steps
Log file
Click Finish to exit.
Finish
To direct input to this virtual machine, press Ctrl+G.

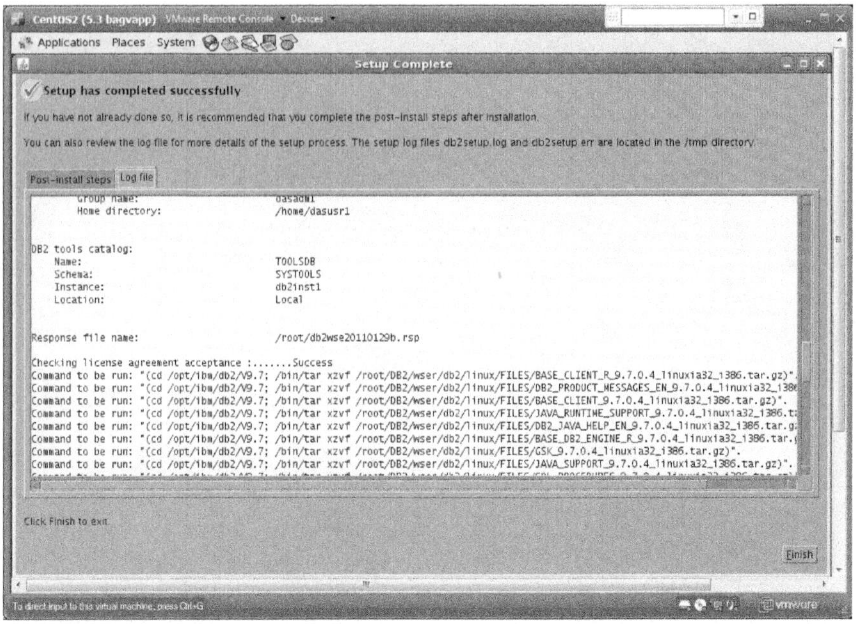

Verify DB2 Installation

Once DB2 is installed, the next step is to verify the installation. The first verification is to change to the db2inst1 user through the following commands:

```
su - db2inst1
```

Next, list the instances and verify db2inst1 shows up:

```
db2ilist
```

Next, try to start the db2 database. (It should complain the database is already started.)

```
db2start
```

Next, list the databases which will only be TOOLDB at this point:

db2 list db directory

Finally, print out the configuration information for the installation.

```
db2 get dbm cfg
```

Summary

After completing these steps, DB2 will be installed successfully.

CONFIGURE icosuser for DB2 [OPTIONAL]

If the icosuser is to be used as the database user instead of or in addition to the db2inst1 user, then additional linkage between the icosuser to the db2inst1 user is required. Enter the following commands to allow icosuser access to the db2 commands:

```
su - db2inst1
chmod 755 /home/db2inst1/sqllib/db2profile
exit
su - icosuser
vi .bashrc
   ADD THE LINE:  .     /home/db2inst1/sqllib/db2profile
exit     ## EXIT AND RE-ENTER IN ORDER TO PICK UP THE PROFILE CHANGE
su - icosuser
db2val
```

These steps can be performed anytime after the DB2 software installation but before the other icosuser configuration steps that occur before the ITNCM core product installation.

CREATE DB2 DATABASE

Introduction

The creation of the DB2 database for ITNCM should be done through the CLI instead of the GUI due to required parameters of the ITNCM product. After the creation the db2inst1 user and the access changes to the db2inst1 (DB2 main user) and optionally the icosuser (ITNCM main user), access to the db2 database is complete.

CLI Creation (correct)

NOTE Using the Control Center Below will not work since we need to have additional columns, etc. This is not currently documented in the ITNCM Installation guide.

So instead use the command:

```
db2 create database ITNCM automatic storage yes pagesize 32768
      dft_extent_sz 32
```

CONFIGURE db2init1 and [optional: icosuser]

Introduction

The ITNCM requires extensions of DB2's regular expression engine. In addition, if the icosuser is to be used as the database user instead of or in addition to the db2inst1 user, then additional linkage between the icosuser to the db2inst1 user is required.

Position ITNCM RegEx Jar for DB2

First untar the ITNCM installation files (if not done already):

```
tar xvf CI3J6EN-Base.tar
```

Within these files there will be the following file:

```
ibm_tivoli-ncm_db2_udf.jar
```

Optionally for ease of reference copy this file to /tmp. (Adjust the commands below accordingly to where file lands.)

```
cd ~/CI3F9EN
cp -p ibm_tivoli-ncm_db2_udf.jar /tmp
chmod 777 /tmp/ibm_*
```

Enable icosuser DB2 Access

If icosuser will be the DB2 user or icosuser will be accessing the DB2 database (and this step wasn't done earlier) enter the following commands to allow icosuser access to the db2 commands:

```
su - db2inst1
chmod 755 /home/db2inst1/sqllib/db2profile
exit
su - icosuser
vi .bashrc
   ADD THE LINE:  .     /home/db2inst1/sqllib/db2profile
exit     ## EXIT AND RE-ENTER IN ORDER TO PICK UP THE PROFILE CHANGE
su - icosuser
db2val
```

Enable ITNCM RegEx Jar for icosuser

Next if the icosuser will be the ITNCM user, then icosuser will also need the regex adaptation ITNCM requires to properly talk to the database. Enter the following commands:

```
db2 CONNECT TO ITNCM USER db2inst1 USING Net-Cool    #(PASSWORD on TEST)
  db2 set current schema=icosuser
  db2 "CALL SQLJ.INSTALL_JAR('file:/tmp/ibm_tivoli-ncm_db2_udf.jar',
ncm_db2_udf)"
  db2 "CALL SQLJ.REFRESH_CLASSES()"
  commit
```

Enable ITNCM RegEx Jar for db2init1

For DB2 default user, also apply the regex changes:

```
su - db2init1
db2 "CALL SQLJ.INSTALL_JAR('file:/tmp/ibm_tivoli-ncm_db2_udf.jar',
      ncm_db2_udf)"
db2 "CALL SQLJ.REFRESH_CLASSES()"
commit
```

The next step is to enable the icosuser to have the proper rights to the ITNCM database:

```
su - db2init1
db2 CONNECT TO ITNCM USER db2inst1 USING Net-Cool    #(PASSWORD on TEST)
db2 "GRANT BINDADD, CONNECT,
CREATE_NOT_FENCED_ROUTINE,CREATE_EXTERNAL_ROUTINE, QUIESCE_CONNECT ON
DATABASE TO USER icosuser"
db2 commit
##db2 connect reset
```

NOTE: The installation guide indicates the DB2 runtime client is required. This is not true if the DB2 server is co-located with the TCR portion of the ITNCM product.

Verify Connection

The final step is to verify a connection can be made to the server for db2inst1:

```
xhost +
su - db2inst1
clpplus
       connect
```

And verify a connection can be made to the server for icosuser:

```
xhost +
su - icosuser
clpplus
       connect
```

The default information is:

```
Database: ITNCM
Host: localhost
Port: 50000
Instance: db2inst1
```

Summary

After completing this section the DB2 database is created and accessible by db2inst1 user and optionally the icosuser user (the primary ITNCM user.)

ITNCM Core Installation

Once the system is prepared and DB2 database is installed, then the core ITNCM product can be installed.

```
su - icosuser
cd BASE
tar xvf CI3J6EN-Base.tar
sh ./ITNCM_linux_ia32.bin
```

The program will run and return the following:

```
Preparing to install...
Extracting the JRE from the installer archive...
Unpacking the JRE...
Extracting the installation resources from the installer archive...
Configuring the installer for this system's environment...

Launching installer...

Preparing CONSOLE Mode Installation...

======================================================================
ITNCM                                            (created with
InstallAnywhere)
----------------------------------------------------------------------




======================================================================
Introduction
------------

InstallAnywhere will guide you through the installation of IBM Tivoli
Netcool Configuration Manager r6.3.0.0-49630-201110132340-aa09.

It is strongly recommended that you quit all programs before continuing
with this installation.

Respond to each prompt to proceed to the next step in the installation.
If you want to change something on a previous step, type 'back'.

You may cancel this installation at any time by typing 'quit'.

PRESS <ENTER> TO CONTINUE:



======================================================================
```

```
    International Program License Agreement

    Part 1 - General Terms

    BY DOWNLOADING, INSTALLING, COPYING, ACCESSING, CLICKING ON AN
    "ACCEPT" BUTTON, OR OTHERWISE USING THE PROGRAM, LICENSEE AGREES TO
    THE TERMS OF THIS AGREEMENT. IF YOU ARE ACCEPTING THESE TERMS ON
    BEHALF OF LICENSEE, YOU REPRESENT AND WARRANT THAT YOU HAVE FULL
    AUTHORITY TO BIND LICENSEE TO THESE TERMS. IF YOU DO NOT AGREE TO
    THESE TERMS,

    - DO NOT DOWNLOAD, INSTALL, COPY, ACCESS, CLICK ON AN "ACCEPT"
BUTTON,
    OR USE THE PROGRAM; AND

    - PROMPTLY RETURN THE UNUSED MEDIA, DOCUMENTATION, AND PROOF OF
    ENTITLEMENT TO THE PARTY FROM WHOM IT WAS OBTAINED FOR A REFUND OF
THE
    AMOUNT PAID. IF THE PROGRAM WAS DOWNLOADED, DESTROY ALL COPIES OF
THE
    PROGRAM.


Press Enter to continue viewing the license agreement, or enter "1" to
   accept the agreement, "2" to decline it, "3" to print it, or "99" to
go back
   to the previous screen.: 1



===============================================================================
ITNCM Prerequisites
-------------------

Please confirm that the prerequisites specified in the installation
guide for
ITNCM 6.3 have been met. Failure to do so may result in an unsuccessful
installation.


  ->1- Confirm
    2- Exit Installation

ENTER THE NUMBER OF THE DESIRED CHOICE, OR PRESS <ENTER> TO ACCEPT THE
   DEFAULT: 1



===============================================================================
Choose Install Directory
------------------------

Where would you like to install?

  Default Install Folder: /opt/IBM/tivoli/netcool/ncm
```

```
ENTER AN ABSOLUTE PATH, OR PRESS <ENTER> TO ACCEPT THE DEFAULT
      :



=======================================================================
Installation
------------

Please indicate if this installation of ITNCM will be integrated into
an
OMNIbus/Network Manager deployment.

  ->1- No - Not Integrated
    2- Yes - Integrated

ENTER THE NUMBER OF THE DESIRED CHOICE, OR PRESS <ENTER> TO ACCEPT THE
   DEFAULT:



=======================================================================
ITNCM Installation
------------------

Please choose the installation option.

ITNCM Only - Tivoli Common Reporting will not be installed.

ITNCM + Reporting - Tivoli Common Reporting will be installed on this
ITNCM
Server.

  ->1- ITNCM only (No Reporting)
    2- ITNCM + Reporting

ENTER THE NUMBER OF THE DESIRED CHOICE, OR PRESS <ENTER> TO ACCEPT THE
   DEFAULT: 2



=======================================================================
Tivoli Common Reporting - TIP Administration User
-------------------------------------------------

Please enter the TIP Administration User Name

TIP Administration User Name (DEFAULT: tipadmin):



=======================================================================
Enter Password
--------------

Please enter the password for the TIP Administration User
```

```
Password::********


===============================================================================
Enter Password Again
--------------------

Please enter the password for the TIP Administration User again

Password::********


===============================================================================
Database Type
-------------

Please choose the Database Type for this ITNCM deployment.

  ->1- Oracle
    2- DB2

ENTER THE NUMBER OF THE DESIRED CHOICE, OR PRESS <ENTER> TO ACCEPT THE
   DEFAULT: 2


===============================================================================
ITNCM Database
--------------

Please enter the requested information regarding your ITNCM DB2
Database.

Database IP address/hostname (DEFAULT: ): 127.0.0.1

Database port (DEFAULT: 50000):

Database Name (DEFAULT: itncm):

Database Alias (DEFAULT: itncm):

DB2 Instance Home Directory on this platform (DEFAULT: /home/db2inst1)
    :

Database User Name (DEFAULT: icosuser):



===============================================================================
Enter Password
--------------

Please enter the password for the ITNCM Database User.
```

```
Password::*********


===============================================================================
Enter Password Again
--------------------

Please enter the password for the ITNCM Database User again.

Password::********



===============================================================================
Embedded IBM WebSphere Application Server
-----------------------------------------

Please enter the requested information necessary to install and
configure the Embedded IBM WebSphere Application Server.

HTTP Port (DEFAULT: 7001):

Secure Port (DEFAULT: 7002):



===============================================================================
ITNCM Root Realm
----------------

Please enter a value for the ITNCM Root Realm.

Root Realm (DEFAULT: ITNCM):



===============================================================================
Enter Password
--------------

Please enter the password for the Intelliden Super User.  (NOTE: This
is a product user created for starting and stopping ITNCM)

Password::******** (PASSWORD)


===============================================================================
Enter Password Again
--------------------

Please enter the password for the Intelliden Super User again.

Password::******** (PASSWORD)
```

```
=========================================================================
FTP Server
----------

Please enter FTP Server details.

FTP Server (DEFAULT: centos2):

FTP User Account (DEFAULT: icosftp):

FTP User Account Directory (DEFAULT: /home/icosftp):



=========================================================================
Enter Password
--------------

Please enter the password for the FTP user account.

Password::********  (PASSWORD)


=========================================================================
Enter Password Again
--------------------

Please enter the password for the FTP user account again.

Password::******** (PASSWORD)


=========================================================================
ITNCM SMTP Server
------------------

Please enter the SMTP Server.

(example smtp.IBM.net)

SMTP Server (DEFAULT: ): ITNCM.company.com



=========================================================================
ITNCM Name
----------

Please enter a unique name for this instance of ITNCM in your network.
```

```
Name (DEFAULT: ): itncm



======================================================================
ITNCM Platform Type
-------------------

Please indicate whether this is a GUI+Worker Server or Worker Server
only.

  ->1- GUI Server + Worker Server
    2- Worker Server

ENTER THE NUMBER OF THE DESIRED CHOICE, OR PRESS <ENTER> TO ACCEPT THE
   DEFAULT:



======================================================================
ITNCM - Active Compliance Core Server
-------------------------------------

Do you wish to enable the Compliance Core on this Server?

  ->1- Compliance Core not active
    2- Compliance Core active

ENTER THE NUMBER OF THE DESIRED CHOICE, OR PRESS <ENTER> TO ACCEPT THE
   DEFAULT: 2



======================================================================
Admin Ports
-----------

Please enter values for the following ports.

If this is the first instance of ITNCM on this platform, accept the
default values.

Admin Port (DEFAULT: 8101):

Log Server Admin Port (DEFAULT: 8102):

Log Server Port (DEFAULT: 8103):

IDT Daemon Port (DEFAULT: 8104):



======================================================================
ITNCM IDT Server
----------------
```

```
Is this the main IDT Daemon Server ?

  ->1- Yes
    2- No

ENTER THE NUMBER OF THE DESIRED CHOICE, OR PRESS <ENTER> TO ACCEPT THE
   DEFAULT:


===============================================================================
Pre-Installation Summary
------------------------

Please Review the Following Before Continuing:

Product Name:
    ITNCM

Install Folder:
    /opt/IBM/tivoli/netcool/ncm

Platform Type
    GUI+Worker Server

Disk Space Information (for Installation Target):
    Required:  923,262,609 bytes
    Available: 11,256,033,280 bytes

PRESS <ENTER> TO CONTINUE:
/bin/bash: indent: command not found


===============================================================================
Installing...
-------------

 [==================|============|==================|===================]
 [------------------|------------|------------------|-------------------]


===============================================================================
Database Schema
---------------

Do you wish to load the Database Schema?

If the Database schema has already been loaded during a previous
installation
of a GUI Server platform this must not be carried out again.

In a distributed system the schema must be loaded from one GUI Server
only!
```

```
Important!
----------
Loading the Database Schema now will remove any existing ITNCM Schema.

The Database Schema can be loaded at a later time by running

/opt/IBM/tivoli/netcool/ncm/bin/utils/database/loadDBSchema.sh

  ->1- Not required/Load later
    2- Load Now

ENTER THE NUMBER OF THE DESIRED CHOICE, OR PRESS <ENTER> TO ACCEPT THE
   DEFAULT: 2



======================================================================
Warning!!!
----------

You have chosen to reload the ITNCM Database schema on WebGUI-TIP-
Server/itncm.

Any existing ITNCM data in this database will be lost.

Are you sure you wish to continue ?

  ->1- No, return to previous step
    2- Yes, continue

ENTER THE NUMBER OF THE DESIRED CHOICE, OR PRESS <ENTER> TO ACCEPT THE
   DEFAULT: 2

======================================================================
Installation Complete
---------------------

ITNCM has been successfully installed to:

/opt/IBM/tivoli/netcool/ncm


PRESS <ENTER> TO EXIT THE INSTALLER:
```

Summary

Once the product has been installed the next step is to install the drivers. The drivers talk to the managed devices.

Standard Driver Installation

Introduction

After the core product is installed, the next step is to install the Standard Drivers.

Verify UNIX Utility Requirements

First verify the dependent tools exist:

```
su - icosuser
which bunzip2
  /usr/bin/bunzip2
which cpio
  /bin/cpio
which sort
  /bin/sort
```

Stop ITNCM

Next, stop the product:

```
/opt/IBM/tivoli/netcool/ncm/bin/itncm.sh stop
```

The program will respond with the following

```
IBM Tivoli Netcool Configuration Manager
----------------------------------------

Stopping GUI Server

Please enter the Intelliden Super User and password if prompted below:

GUI Server = NOT RUNNING

Stopping Worker Server
Worker Server = NOT RUNNING

Stopping Compliance Server
Compliance Server = NOT RUNNING

Stopping Reporting Server

Please enter the TIP Administration User and password if prompted
below:

Detected Linux RedHat 5
Applying LD_PRELOAD workaround. Ignore any subsequent errors
referencing libfreetype.so
ERROR: ld.so: object '/usr/lib/libfreetype.so.6' from LD_PRELOAD cannot
be preloaded: ignored.
```

```
Using /opt/IBM/tivoli/netcool/ncm/tipv2/java/jre/bin/java
ERROR: ld.so: object '/usr/lib/libfreetype.so.6' from LD_PRELOAD cannot
be preloaded: ignored.
ERROR: ld.so: object '/usr/lib/libfreetype.so.6' from LD_PRELOAD cannot
be preloaded: ignored.
ERROR: ld.so: object '/usr/lib/libfreetype.so.6' from LD_PRELOAD cannot
be preloaded: ignored.
ADMU0116I: Tool information is being logged in file

/opt/IBM/tivoli/netcool/ncm/tipv2/profiles/TIPProfile/logs/server1/stop
Server.log
ADMU0128I: Starting tool with the TIPProfile profile
ADMU3100I: Reading configuration for server: server1
ADMU0509I: The server "server1" cannot be reached. It appears to be
stopped.
ADMU0211I: Error details may be seen in the file:

/opt/IBM/tivoli/netcool/ncm/tipv2/profiles/TIPProfile/logs/server1/stop
Server.log
Reporting Server = NOT RUNNING
```

Install Standard Drivers

After the product is stopped, then the files are deployed and drivers installed:

```
cd TNCM-Install/
mkdir STANDARD
mv CI3F2EN-Drivers.tar STANDARD/
cd STANDARD/
tar xvf CI3F2EN-Drivers.tar
```

The tar command will take a few minutes to unbundle the following:

```
Disk1/
Disk1/InstData/
Disk1/InstData/MediaId.properties
Disk1/InstData/Resource1-part3.zip
Disk1/InstData/Resource1.zip
Disk1/InstData/Resource1-part2.zip
Disk1/InstData/ITNCMDrivers.bin
ITNCM_Drivers14_Readme.doc
```

Next the standard driver installer is run:

```
sh ./Disk1/InstData/ITNCMDrivers.bin LAX_VM
      /opt/IBM/tivoli/netcool/ncm/jre/bin/java -i console
```

This results in the following dialog:

```
Preparing to install...
Extracting the installation resources from the installer archive...
Configuring the installer for this system's environment...

Launching installer...
```

```
Preparing CONSOLE Mode Installation...

===============================================================================
ITNCMDrivers                                            (created with
InstallAnywhere)
-------------------------------------------------------------------------------




===============================================================================
Introduction
------------

You will be guided through the installation of IBM Tivoli Netcool
Configuration Manager Drivers support version 6.3.0.2.

It is strongly recommended that you quit all programs before continuing
with this installation.

Respond to each prompt to proceed to the next step in the installation.
If you want to change something on a previous step, type 'back'.

You may cancel this installation at any time by typing 'quit'.

PRESS <ENTER> TO CONTINUE:



===============================================================================
Choose Install Set
------------------

Please choose the Install Set to be installed by this installer.

  ->1- All Devices
    2- ACME Devices
    3- Actelis Devices
    4- Adtran Devices
    5- Alcatel Devices
    6- Arris Devices
    7- Cisco Devices
    8- Extreme Devices
    9- Foundry Devices
   10- Harmonic Devices
   11- Huawei Devices
   12- IBM Devices
   13- IBM-BNT Devices
   14- Itron Devices
   15- Juniper Devices
   16- Lucent Devices
   17- MRV Devices
   18- NokiaSiemens Devices
   19- Nortel Devices
   20- RAD Devices
   21- Tellabs Devices
   22- VMware Devices
```

```
   23- World Wide Packets

   24- Customize...

ENTER THE NUMBER FOR THE INSTALL SET, OR PRESS <ENTER> TO ACCEPT THE
DEFAULT
   : 7


===============================================================================



    International Program License Agreement

    Part 1 - General Terms

    BY DOWNLOADING, INSTALLING, COPYING, ACCESSING, CLICKING ON AN
    "ACCEPT" BUTTON, OR OTHERWISE USING THE PROGRAM, LICENSEE AGREES TO
    THE TERMS OF THIS AGREEMENT. IF YOU ARE ACCEPTING THESE TERMS ON
    BEHALF OF LICENSEE, YOU REPRESENT AND WARRANT THAT YOU HAVE FULL
    AUTHORITY TO BIND LICENSEE TO THESE TERMS. IF YOU DO NOT AGREE TO
    THESE TERMS,

    - DO NOT DOWNLOAD, INSTALL, COPY, ACCESS, CLICK ON AN "ACCEPT"
BUTTON,
    OR USE THE PROGRAM; AND

    - PROMPTLY RETURN THE UNUSED MEDIA, DOCUMENTATION, AND PROOF OF
    ENTITLEMENT TO THE PARTY FROM WHOM IT WAS OBTAINED FOR A REFUND OF
THE
    AMOUNT PAID. IF THE PROGRAM WAS DOWNLOADED, DESTROY ALL COPIES OF
THE
    PROGRAM.


Press Enter to continue viewing the license agreement, or enter "1" to
   accept the agreement, "2" to decline it, "3" to print it, or "99" to
go back
   to the previous screen.: 1



===============================================================================
Pre-Installation Summary
------------------------

Please Review the Following Before Continuing:

Product Name:
    ITNCMDrivers

Install Folder:
    /opt/IBM/tivoli/netcool/ncm
```

```
Product Components:
    Firewall,
    5xx,
    6.x,
    FWSM,
    3.x,
    Hub,
    15xx,
    1.01,
    Router,
    C10K-P10-MZ-12.0-27-S1,
    100xx,
    12.2-x,
    107xx,
    C10700-P-M-120-24.S1,
    12xxx,
    GSR-K4P-M-12.0-30S,
    16xx,
    11.x-x,
    C1600-OSY56I-M-12.0-28A,
    C1600-K8OSY-M-12.2-26,
    17xx,
    C1700-K9O3SV8Y7-M-12.3-10,
    24xx,
    12.3-x,
    26xx,
    11.x-x,
    C2600-IK9O3S-M-12.2-21a,
    C2600-IK9O3S-M-12.3-9,
    C2600-IS-M-12.0,
    36xx,
    11.x-x,
    C3600-IK903S-M-12.2,
    C3640-IK9S-MZ.123-6A,
    C3640-JS-MZ-12.0,
    37xx,
    C3745-J-MZ-12.2,
    C3745-IK9S-M-12.3-6,
    72xx,
    11.x-x,
    C7200-P-M-12.0-23-S1,
    C7200-P-M-12.1-14-E3,
    C7200-P-M-12.2-13b,
    73xx,
    c7301-ik9s-mz-123-5,
    75xx,
    11.x-x,
    RSP-PV-M-12.1-14-E1,
    RSP-PV-M-12.2-13b,
    76xx,
    12.1-x,
    Switch,
    154xx,
    4.6.1,
    2950-xx,
    C2950-C3H2S-MZ-12.0-5-3WC1,
```

```
C2950-I6Q4L2-M-12.1-13-EA1b,
29xx,
C2900XL-C3H2S-M-12.0-5-WC8,
C2940-I6Q4L2-MZ.121-22.EA1,
35xx,
C3550-I5Q3L2-M-12.1-19-EA1,
40xx,
4.x-x,
6.3.6,
55xx,
4.x-x,
5.5.14,
6.3.6,
65xx,
6.3.6,
7.4.3,
8.2.2,
LANE,
12.0-26-W5-28a,
12.1-5c-E10,
32xx,
C3200-I11K9-MZ.122-15.ZL,
S72033-PK9SV-MZ.12.2-17D-SXB5,
C7200-IK9S-M-12.3-12a,
53xx,
C5300-IK9S-M-12.3-13,
RSM,
12.0-x,
C3550-I5Q3L2-M-12.2-25-SEA,
C5300-IS56I-MZ-12.0-28c,
RSP-K4PV-M-12.0-30-S2,
RSP-PV-MZ-12.3-9,
28xx,
C2800NM-ADVIPSERVICESK9-M-12.4-1a,
C5RSM-ISV-MZ-12.1-25,
12.4-x,
C2800NM-ADVIPSERVICESK9-12.4T,
7.6.13,
CMTS,
UBR72xx,
UBR7200-IK8S-MZ-12.2-15-BC2G,
SCA,
11000,
4.2,
C7200-P-MZ.12.4-3b,
C2600-ADVIPSERVICESK9-MZ-12.4-5a,
Content Switch,
11xxx,
6.x,
SB10x,
SB106-K9OY1-MZ-12.4-7,
8xx,
C870-ADVIPSERVICESK9-MZ-12.4-4XC1,
CRSx,
3.3.x,
UBR7200-IK9SU2-M-12.3-21-BC,
asa55xx,
```

```
    7.x,
    8.x,
    AP12xx,
    12.3-x,
    MEXX,
    MEXXME340X-METROIPACCESSK9-M.122-35-SE3,
    12.4-x,
    ACE,
    ACE,
    3.x,
    3.3.x,
    12.3-x,
    C1700-ADVIPSERVICESK9-M.124-13,
    C36xx-12.4,
    RSP-IK9O3SV-MZ-12.4-17,
    8.4.11,
    C7200-12.4T,
    CAT4000-I9K91S-MZ-12.2-25.EWA12,
    45xx,
    CAT4000-I9K91S-MZ-12.2-25.EWA12,
    12.1-x,
    12.1-x,
    12.4-x,
    7.x,
    A2,
    12.4-x,
    CGESM,
    12.1,
    12.2,
    Cisco,
    4.x,
    15.0-x,
    ASR,
    2.4.x,
    nexus4k,
    4.x,
    15.0-x,
    ISRG2,
    15.x,
    5.x


PRESS <ENTER> TO CONTINUE:



===============================================================================
Installing...
-------------

 [==================|=================|=================|=================]
 [------------------|-----------------|-----------------|-----------------]



===============================================================================
```

```
Installation Complete
---------------------

Congratulations. IBM Tivoli Netcool Configuration Manager Drivers
support
version 6.3.0.2 has been successfully installed.

PRESS <ENTER> TO EXIT THE INSTALLER:
```

Start ITNCM

Next the product is started:

```
/opt/IBM/tivoli/netcool/ncm/bin/itncm.sh start
```

The following is the response:

```
IBM Tivoli Netcool Configuration Manager
----------------------------------------
Starting Worker Server
Worker Server = RUNNING

Starting Compliance Server
Compliance Server = RUNNING

Starting GUI Server
GUI Server = RUNNING

Starting Reporting Server
Reporting Server = RUNNING
```

NOTE: The Out of Band Control (OOBC) daemon to be installed later in this document does NOT use this same script. As a result the /etc/init.d/itncm script that is installed later in this document needs to be manually modified to include oobc.sh. This modified script appears in the Appendix.

Verify Drivers

Next, verify the drivers are working:

```
/opt/IBM/tivoli/netcool/ncm/bin/utils/driverTools.sh -status
```

The response should be as follows:

```
Loading driver information from database...
Installation OK! All servers are running the same drivers installation.
----------------------------------------------------------------
  Server    |  Status
----------------------------------------------------------------
  itncm     |  Consistent (Max=Isd0000104154)
----------------------------------------------------------------
```

Smart Driver Installation

Introduction

After the standard drivers are installed, the more advanced Smart Drivers should be installed.

Place Smart Drivers

The following steps were performed to place and untar the installation file for the smart driver:

```
su - icosuser
mkdir SMART
mv CI3F5EN-SmartModel.tar  SMART/
cd SMART/
tar xvf CI3F5EN-SmartModel.tar
```

The following folders and files will be created from the tar:

```
Disk1/
Disk1/InstData/
Disk1/InstData/MediaId.properties
Disk1/InstData/Resource1-part3.zip
Disk1/InstData/Resource1.zip
Disk1/InstData/Resource1-part2.zip
Disk1/InstData/ITNCMDrivers.bin
ITNCM_Drivers14_Readme.doc
ITNCMSmartModelTier2Upgrade.bin
```

Install Smart Drivers

Next, the installation program is run:

```
sh ./ITNCMSmartModelTier2Upgrade.bin LAX_VM
      /opt/IBM/tivoli/netcool/ncm/jre/bin/java -i console
```

The following dialog results from this installation:

```
Preparing to install...
Extracting the installation resources from the installer archive...
Configuring the installer for this system's environment...

Launching installer...

Preparing CONSOLE Mode Installation...

===============================================================================
ITNCMSmartModelTier2Upgrade                              (created with
InstallAnywhere)
-------------------------------------------------------------------------------
```

```
===============================================================================
Introduction
------------

You are about to install IBM Tivoli Netcool Configuration Manager -
Drivers
ITNCMSmartModelTier2Upgrade version 6.3.0.2.  It is strongly
recommended that
you quit all programs before continuing with this installation.
Respond to
each prompt to proceed to the next step in the installation.  If you
want to
change something on a previous step, type 'back'.  You may cancel this
installation at any time by typing 'quit'.

PRESS <ENTER> TO CONTINUE:



===============================================================================



    International Program License Agreement

    Part 1 - General Terms

    BY DOWNLOADING, INSTALLING, COPYING, ACCESSING, CLICKING ON AN
    "ACCEPT" BUTTON, OR OTHERWISE USING THE PROGRAM, LICENSEE AGREES TO
    THE TERMS OF THIS AGREEMENT. IF YOU ARE ACCEPTING THESE TERMS ON
    BEHALF OF LICENSEE, YOU REPRESENT AND WARRANT THAT YOU HAVE FULL
    AUTHORITY TO BIND LICENSEE TO THESE TERMS. IF YOU DO NOT AGREE TO
    THESE TERMS,

    - DO NOT DOWNLOAD, INSTALL, COPY, ACCESS, CLICK ON AN "ACCEPT"
BUTTON,
    OR USE THE PROGRAM; AND

    - PROMPTLY RETURN THE UNUSED MEDIA, DOCUMENTATION, AND PROOF OF
    ENTITLEMENT TO THE PARTY FROM WHOM IT WAS OBTAINED FOR A REFUND OF
THE
    AMOUNT PAID. IF THE PROGRAM WAS DOWNLOADED, DESTROY ALL COPIES OF
THE
    PROGRAM.


Press Enter to continue viewing the license agreement, or enter "1" to
   accept the agreement, "2" to decline it, "3" to print it, or "99" to
go back
   to the previous screen.:1
```

```
===============================================================================
Pre-Installation Summary
------------------------

Please Review the Following Before Continuing:

Product Name:
    ITNCMSmartModelTier2Upgrade

Install Folder:
    /opt/IBM/tivoli/netcool/ncm

Java VM to be Used by Installed Product:
    /opt/IBM/tivoli/netcool/ncm/eWAS/java

Disk Space Information (for Installation Target):
    Required:  73,253,541 bytes
    Available: 56,444,350,464 bytes

PRESS <ENTER> TO CONTINUE:



===============================================================================
Installing...
-------------

 [==================|================|===============|===============]
 [------------------|----------------|---------------|---------------]



===============================================================================
Installation Complete
---------------------

Congratulations. ITNCMSmartModelTier2Upgrade version 6.3.0.2 has been
successfully installed.

PRESS <ENTER> TO EXIT THE INSTALLER:
```

Upgrade Existing Drivers to Smart Drivers

Now that the smart drivers have been deployed the upgrade utility needs to be run:

```
cd /opt/IBM/tivoli/netcool/ncm/drivers/bin/
./smartModelTier2Upgrade.sh -all
```

The following dialog results:

```
--------------------------------
  Smart Model Tier 2 Upgrade
--------------------------------
Enabled SmartModel mode for all drivers. Please restart all servers.
```

```
[icosuser@tncm-001 bin]$ cd  /opt/IBM/tivoli/netcool/ncm/bin/
[icosuser@tncm-001 bin]$ ./itncm.sh start


IBM Tivoli Netcool Configuration Manager
----------------------------------------
Starting Worker Server
Worker Server = RUNNING

Starting Compliance Server
Compliance Server = RUNNING

Starting GUI Server
GUI Server = RUNNING

Starting Reporting Server
Reporting Server = RUNNING
```

Summary

Now that the smart driver is deployed the ITNCM product needs to be configured.

Configuring ITNCM (Command line)

Introduction

Several steps were required to configure the ITNCM application. Several of these were done from the command line.

Skipped Steps

The following steps were not needed:

- Run schema creation (done as part of install and correction afterwards.)
- Increase JAVA heap memory size. (Not needed due to small installation.)
- HTTP Connection setup. (Not required.)
- Configuring a backup presentation server. (Doesn't exist.)
- Change platform configuration. (Not required.)
- Enabling/Disabiling FIPS 140-2 Mode. (Not required.)

However, other options were needed. The implementation of these options are detailed here:

Add House keeping

The following command was executed to add housekeeping:

```
vi /opt/IBM/tivoli/netcool/ncm/config/server/config.xml
Append to end:
        <component>
                <name>InternalHousekeepingComponent</name>

<class>com.intelliden.internalhousekeeping.InternalHousekeepingComponen
t</class>
        </component>
```

Adding autostart capability

ITNCM is configured to restart by running the appropriate script:

```
su -
cd /opt/IBM/tivoli/netcool/ncm/bin/utils/
./createAutoStart.sh
      itncm          0:off    1:off    2:on     3:on     4:on     5:on
      6:off
ls -l /etc/init.d/itncm
      -rwxr-xr-x 1 root root 821 Feb  2 10:48 /etc/init.d/itncm
```

NOTE: Autostart does NOT include the OOBC daemon. Also there are bugs in the script that is created. See the Appendices for the correct script that fixes these bugs and includes OOBC in the auto start and stop.

Import Standard Compliance Policies

Policies are used by ITNCM to measure variances of network device configurations against standards. Some standard policies have been created by IBM (Intelliden.) They were imported using the following process two step process.

First, the sample policies were copied into place and deployed.

```
cp -p
/opt/IBM/tivoli/netcool/ncm/compliance/db/export/samplePolicies/sample_
policies.tar /opt/IBM/tivoli/netcool/ncm/compliance/db/export/tables/
cd /opt/IBM/tivoli/netcool/ncm/compliance/db/export/tables/
      tar xvf sample_policies.tar
      alarmaction.xml
      commandsetaction.xml
      definition.xml
      emailaction.xml
      evaluation.xml
      extraction.xml
      globalparameter.xml
      parametergroupvalue.xml
      parametergroup.xml
      policytoalarmaction.xml
      policytoemailaction.xml
      policytorule.xml
      policy.xml
      ruleblob.xml
      ruletocommandsetaction.xml
      ruletodefinition.xml
      rule.xml
```

Second, the deployed policies were imported into ITNCM:

```
cd /opt/IBM/tivoli/netcool/ncm/compliance/bin/utils/
./dbImport.sh
      Importing table: policy
      Importing 23 rows into table policy
      Importing table: policytorule
      Importing 26 rows into table policytorule
      Importing table: rule
      Importing 26 rows into table rule
      Importing table: ruleblob
      Importing 26 rows into table ruleblob
      Importing table: ruletodefinition
      Importing 58 rows into table ruletodefinition
      Importing table: definition
      Importing 58 rows into table definition
      Importing table: evaluation
```

```
Importing 258 rows into table evaluation
Importing table: alarmaction
Importing 0 rows into table alarmaction
Importing table: emailaction
Importing 0 rows into table emailaction
Importing table: policytoalarmaction
Importing 0 rows into table policytoalarmaction
Importing table: policytoemailaction
Importing 0 rows into table policytoemailaction
Importing table: commandsetaction
Importing 0 rows into table commandsetaction
Importing table: ruletocommandsetaction
Importing 0 rows into table ruletocommandsetaction
Importing table: globalparameter
Importing 0 rows into table globalparameter
Importing table: extraction
Importing 0 rows into table extraction
Importing table: extractiontoxpath
File does not exist - no entries imported
Importing table: parametergroup
Importing 0 rows into table parametergroup
Importing table: parametergroupvalue
Importing 0 rows into table parametergroupvalue
Importing table: scriptparameter
File does not exist - no entries imported
Importing table: evaluationparam
File does not exist - no entries imported
Done
```

NOTE: Tthese policies will not appear until through the ITNCM Compliance GUI the policies are associated to an administrative user. This step is done AFTER the ITNCM GUI Verification step.

Summary

After the initial command line based configuration, the next step is to validate the installation of ITNCM by logging into the GUI.

Verify ITCNM GUI

Introduction

After some initial configuration from the command line, the next step is to validate the ITNCM installation by logging onto the TCR/TIP (reporting) and ITNCM (core application) interfaces via the Internet browser.

TCR/TIP Verification

Log onto TIP through the browser using http:/WebGUI-TIP-Server:16310/ibm/console using tipadmin and PASSWORD as username and password.

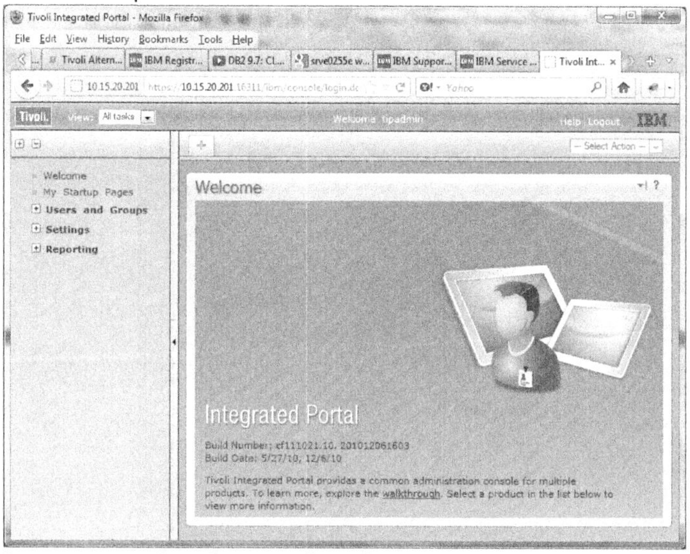

Select all Roles except SuppressMonitor for TipAdmin by going to Users and Groups->User Roles. Then click search and click on the link TipAdmin in the table listing. Then click on all the listed roles except for suppressmonitor.

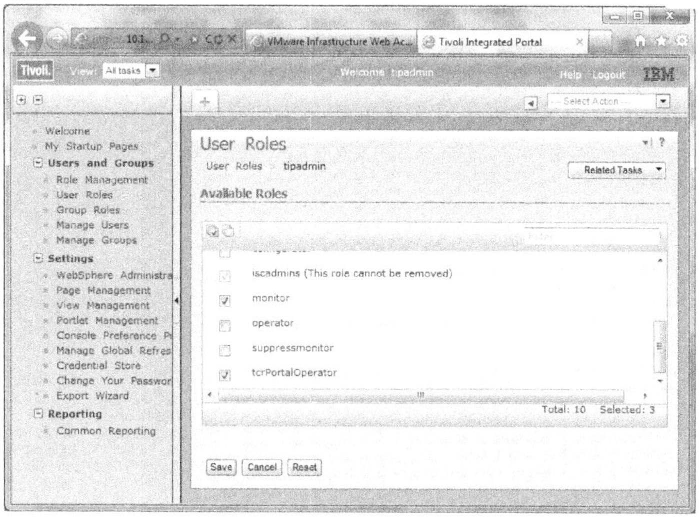

Click Save and once the screen returns to the User list click logout and log back into TIP.

ITNCM Portal

Log into ITNCM via http://WebGUI-TIP-Server:7001 and use Intelliden and PASSWORD as the username and password. (This is the Super User information inputed during installation.)

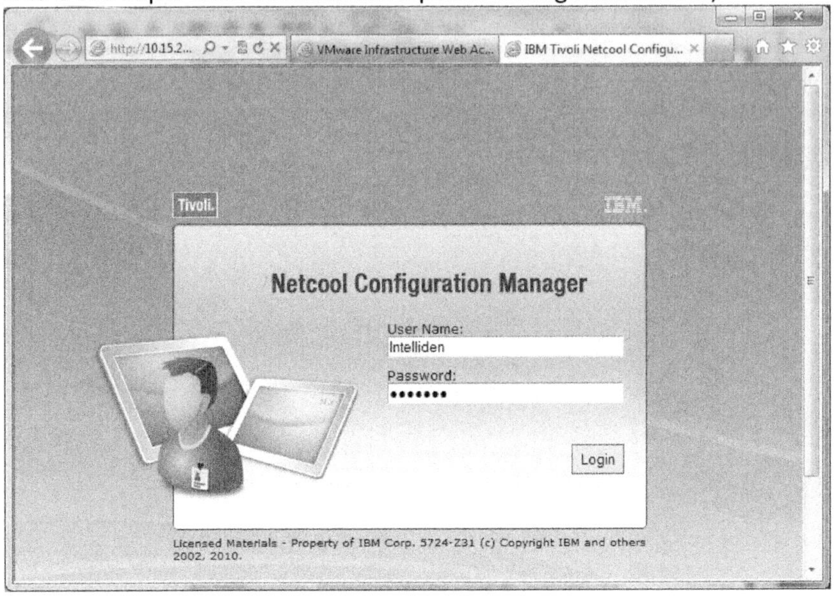

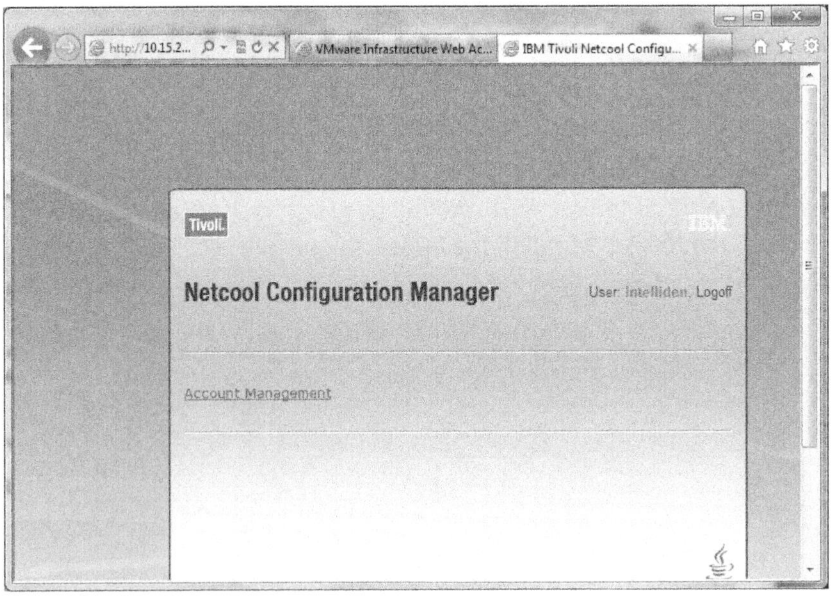

Now log off.

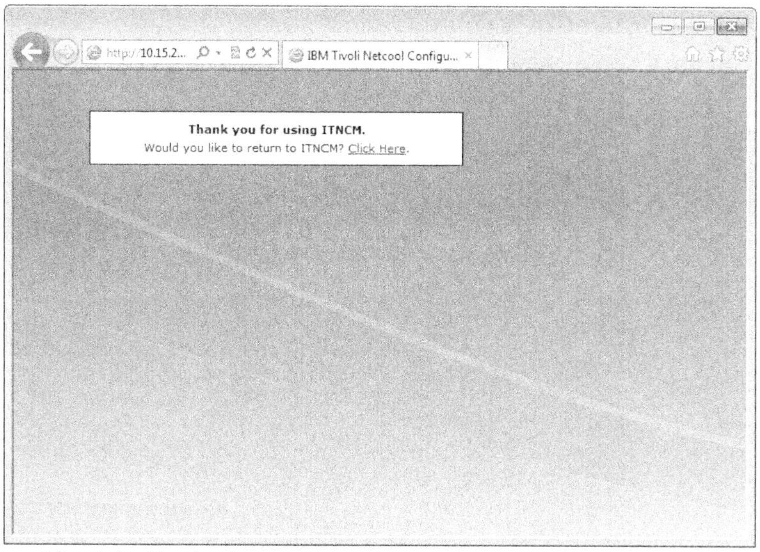

Next click the link to get back to the login page.

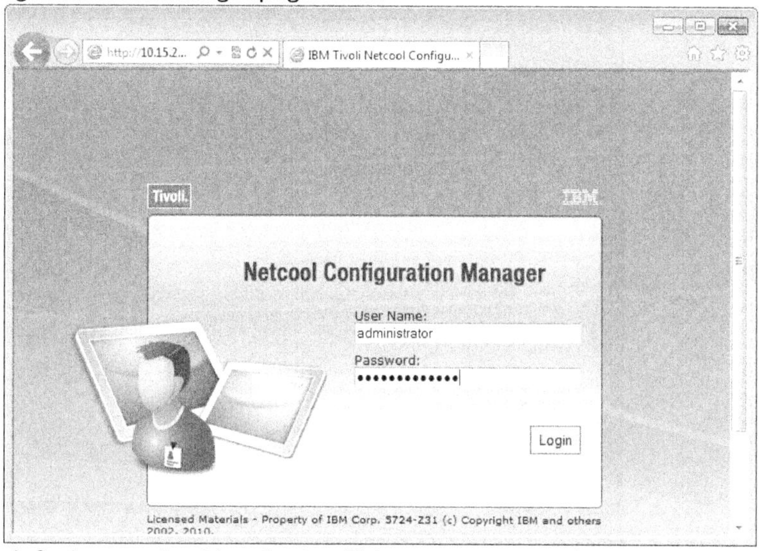

Intelliden has three default users besides the Intelliden super user: administrator, observer, and operator. The passwords for these users are the same as their usernames.

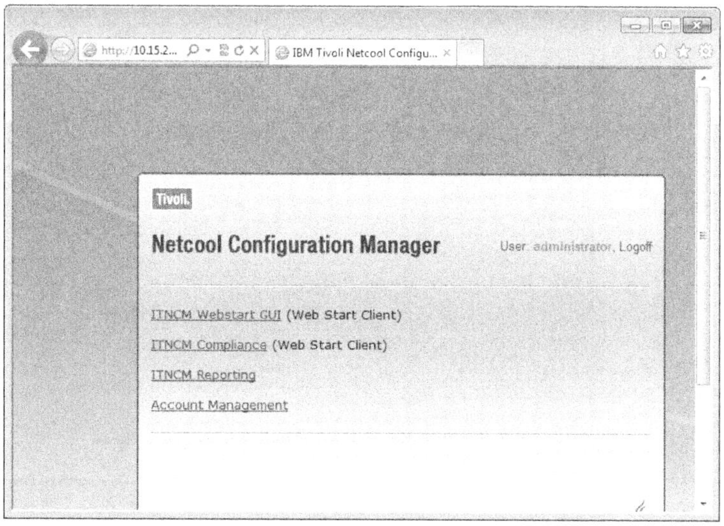

Next, click on the ITNCM Webstart GUI to verify that the primary GUI can be accessed and JAVA is correctly configured on the desktop system.

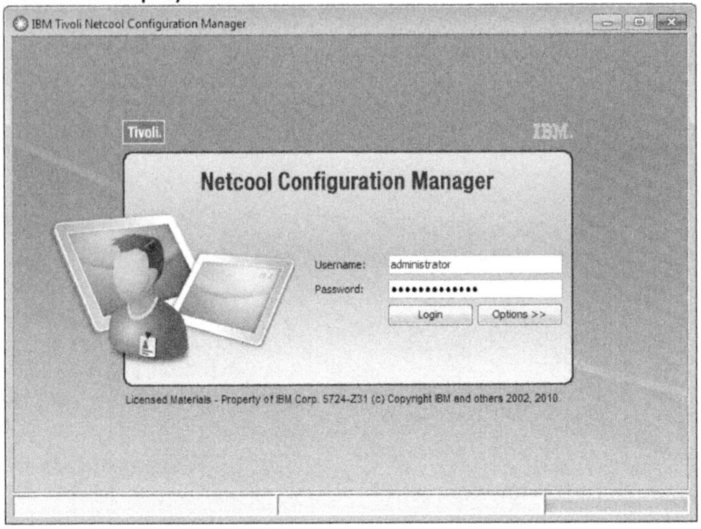

Enter the administrator credentials again.

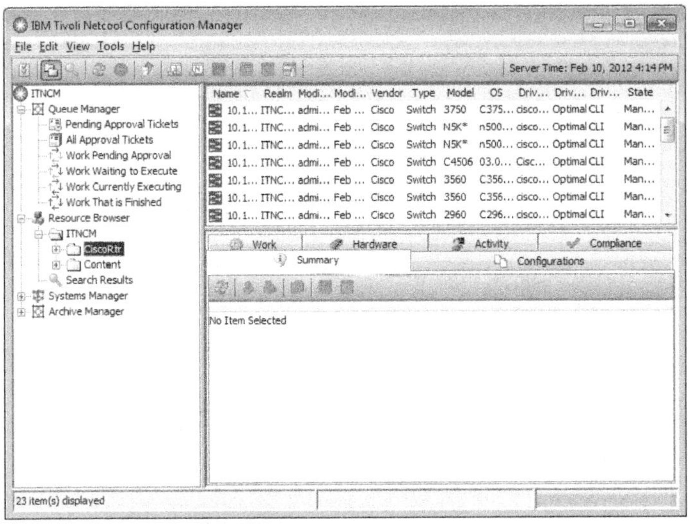

Summary

These step will verify that ITNCM is correctly installed and that the local JAVA client and browser used to access the server are correctly configured.

Configure ITNCM via the GUI

Introduction

After the product has been installed, the initial command line configuration complete, and the GUI has been accessed, the next step is to configure the rest of the product. The following steps configure ITNCM via the GUI.

Start the ITNCM GUI (Core)

Now login as administrator/administrator and get the following screen

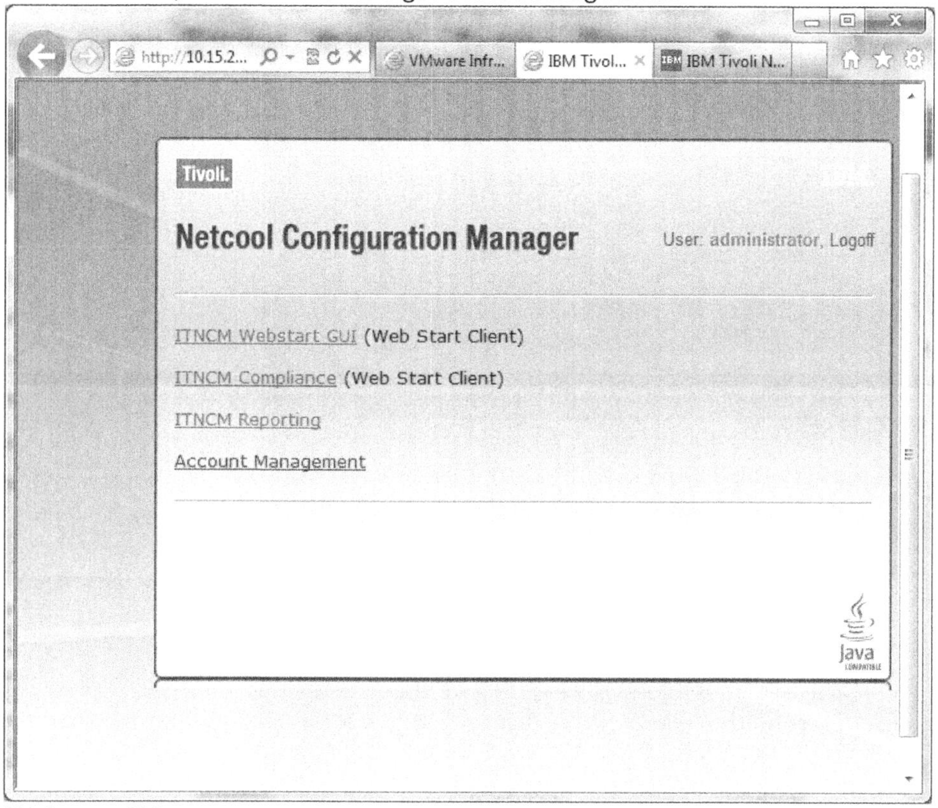

Click ITNCM Webstart GUI

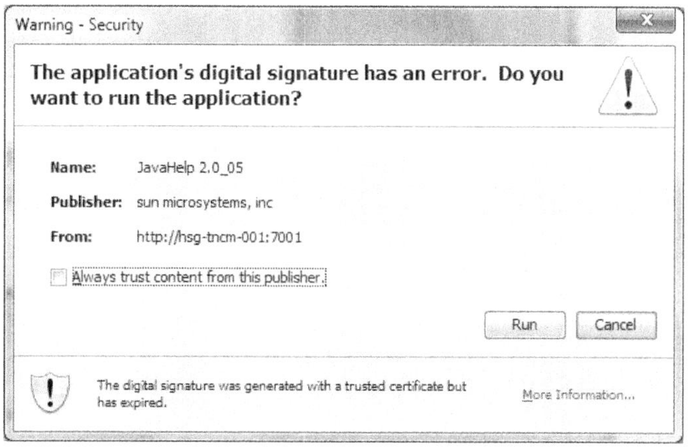

Click the check box and RUN.

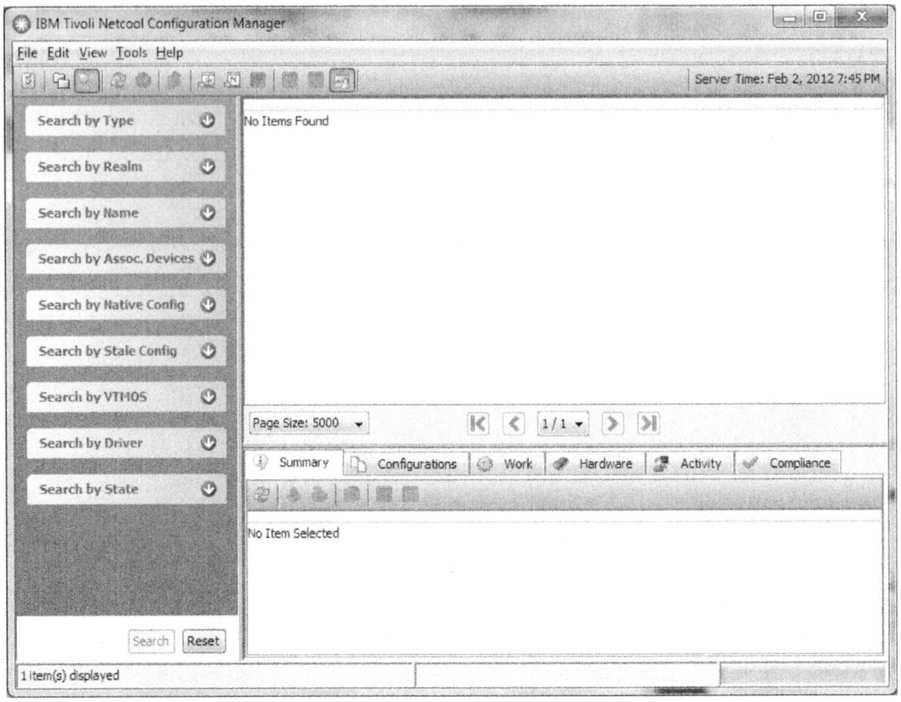

Set Timezone

Set the timezone by selecting File->Preferences and click User Information in the new window

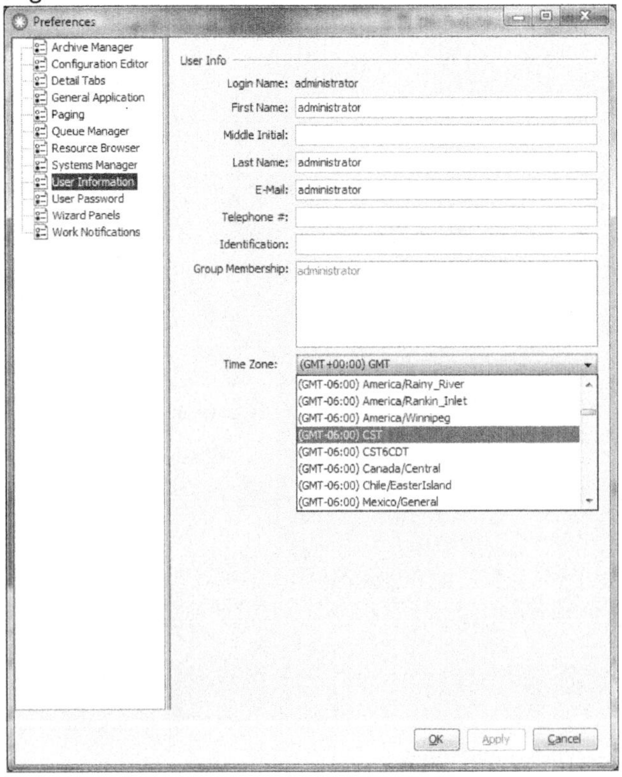

Set Resource Visibility

Next select resources

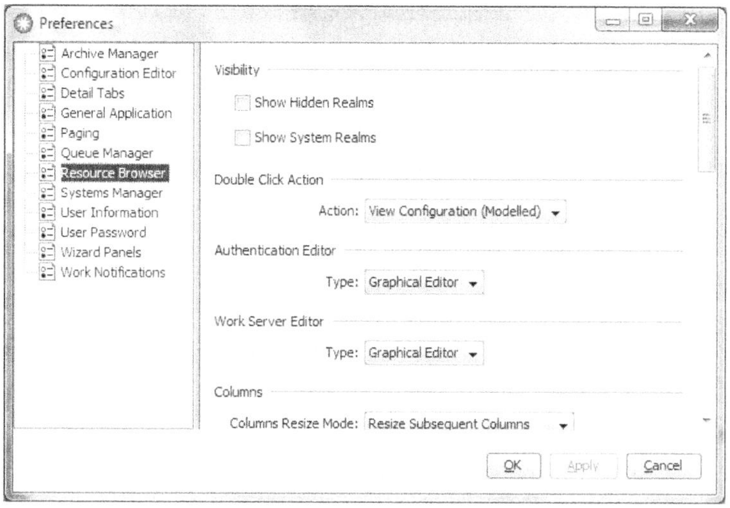

Show everything

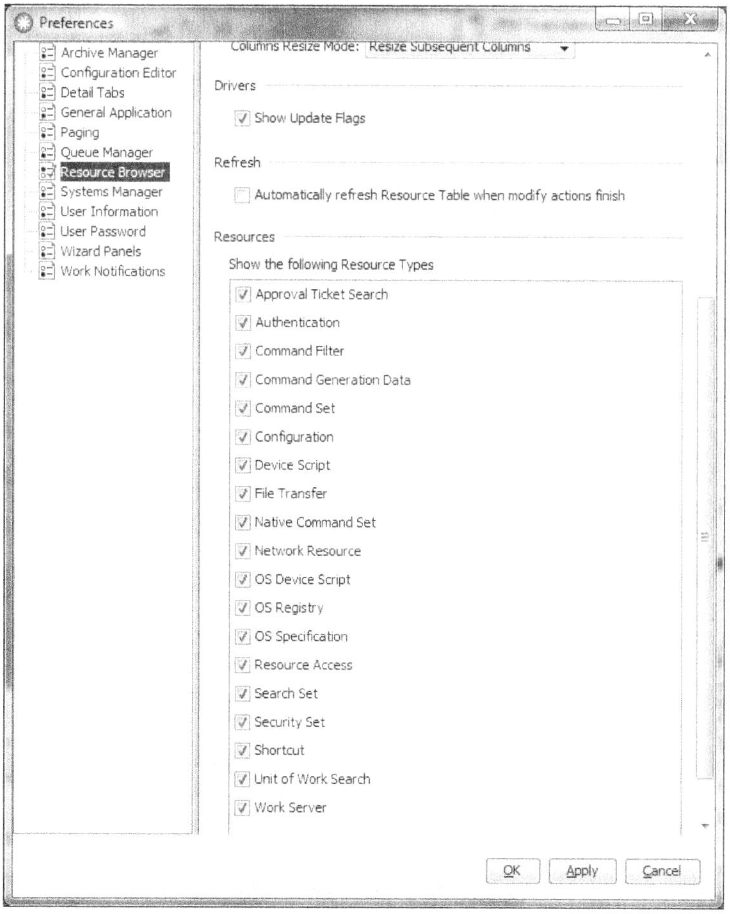

Configure the Worker Server Resource

Set up Worker Server. These servers do all the heavy lifting between ITNCM and the managed network devices. They perform telnet/ssh sessions, back up configurations, etc.

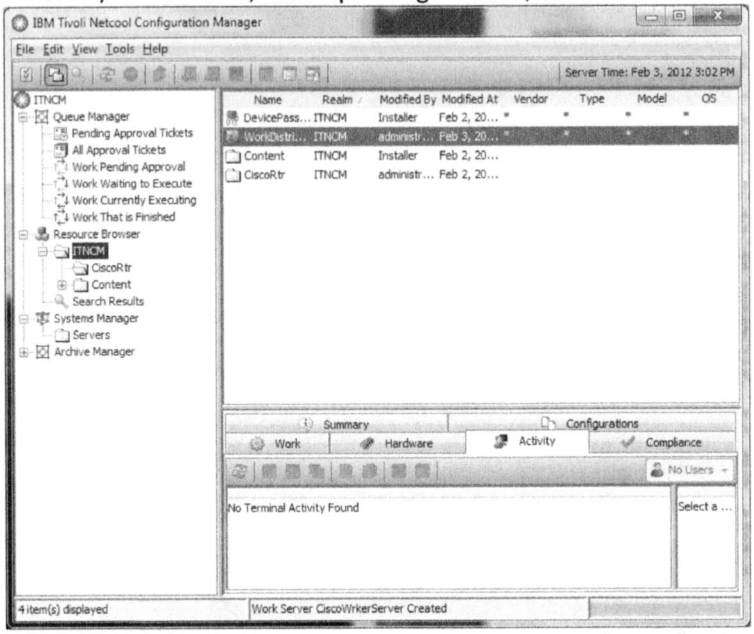

Make sure the folder icon is selected in the top ribbon and that the top "realm", which is ITNCM, is highlighted above. If so, then right click on WorkDistribution and select edit

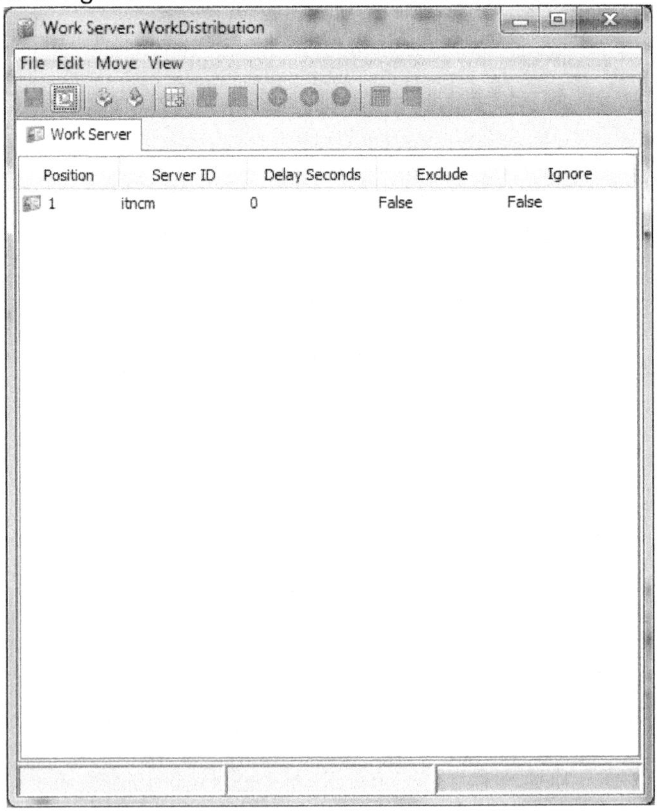

Delete the last two entries and right click on the first entry and select edit and adjust the values accordingly

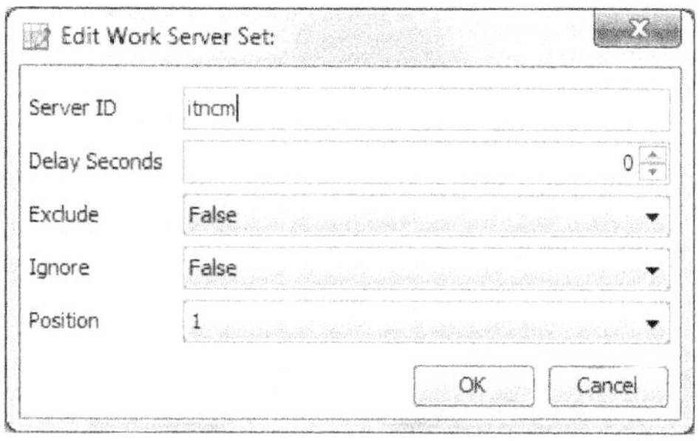

NOTE Make sure Ignore and Exclude are both set to FALSE.

Click OK. In the WorkServer: Work Distribution form, click the Disk Icon to save the configuration and click File->Close to exit.

Configure Device Passwords

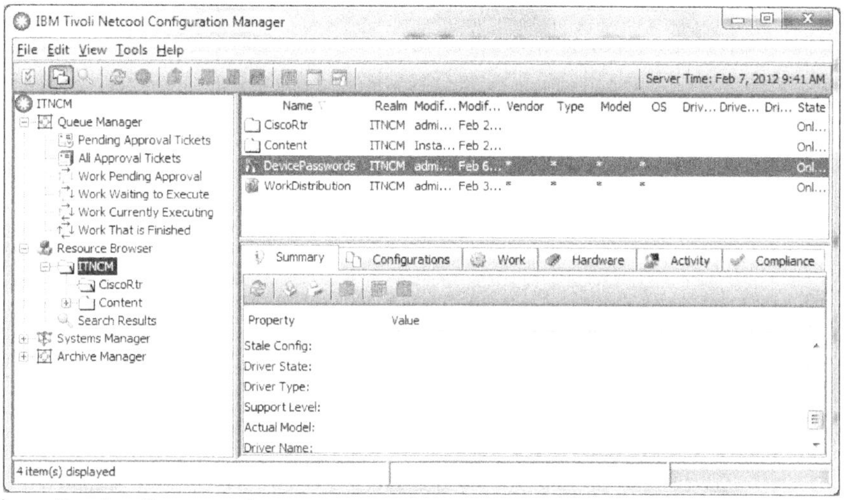

Next double click on Device Passwords

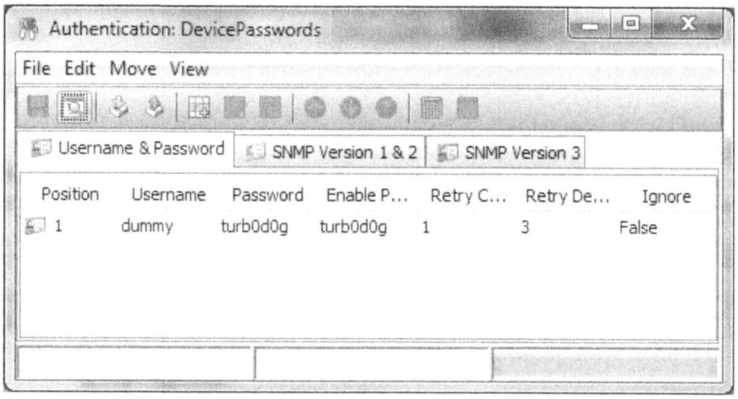

Then double lick and modify the entries accordingly

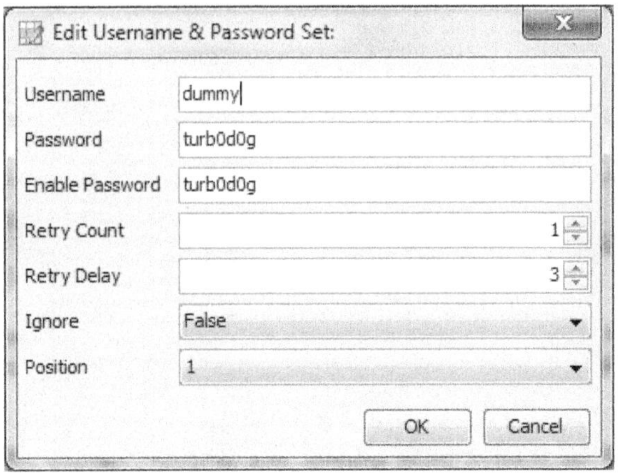

NOTE:

1. Make sure to enter a Username even though it isn't used by the router. This is due to a parsing bug in the ITNCM application.
2. Make sure to set Ignore to False. Otherwise it will ignore the entry. By default it is False so this entry has to be changed.

Once the values are entered correctly click OK.

In the Authentication:Passwords menu click the Disk Icon to save the configuration and click File->Close to exit.

Create top Realm

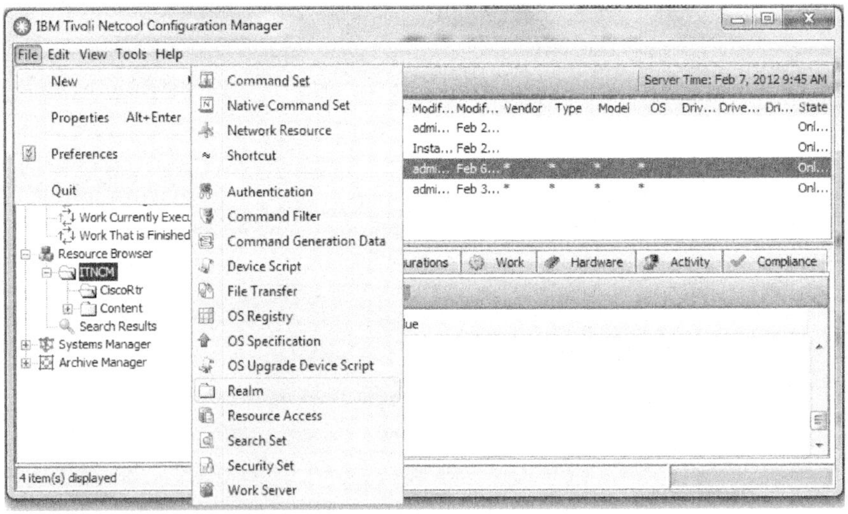

Next create a top realm by selecting File->New->Realm

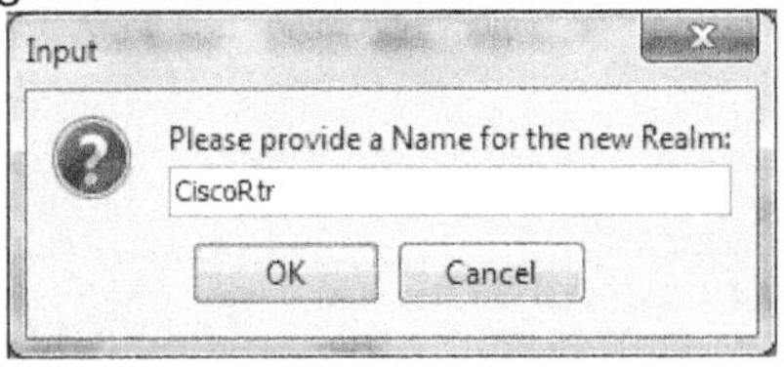

Enter the name of the realm and click OK.

Create New Worker Server in the New Realm

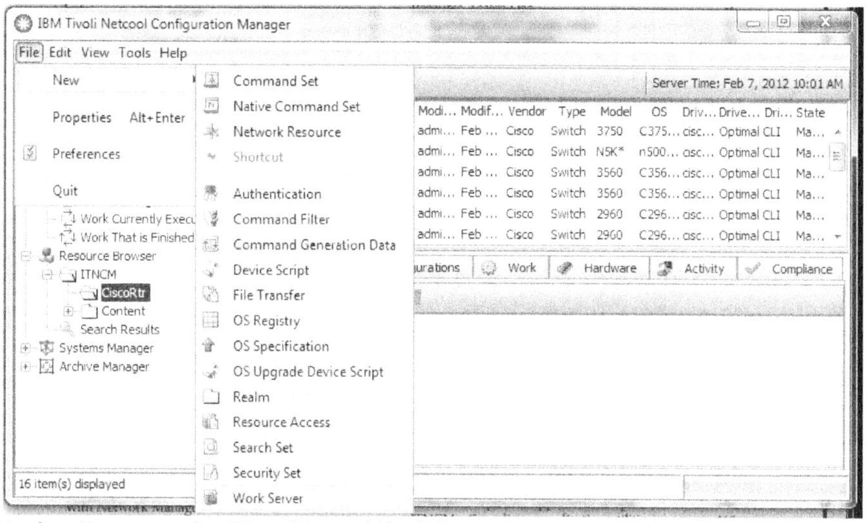

Create a new Worker Resource by File->New->Work Server

Fill out the form and click OK.

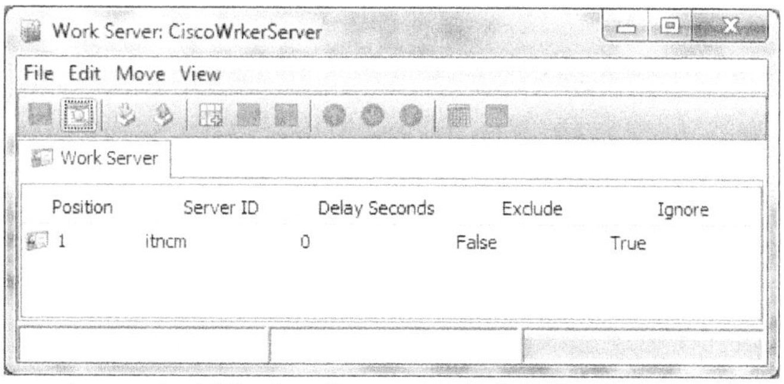

Next double click on the newly created Worker Server and click the Add Icon (spreadsheet with the plus symbol in the ribbon beneath the menu.)

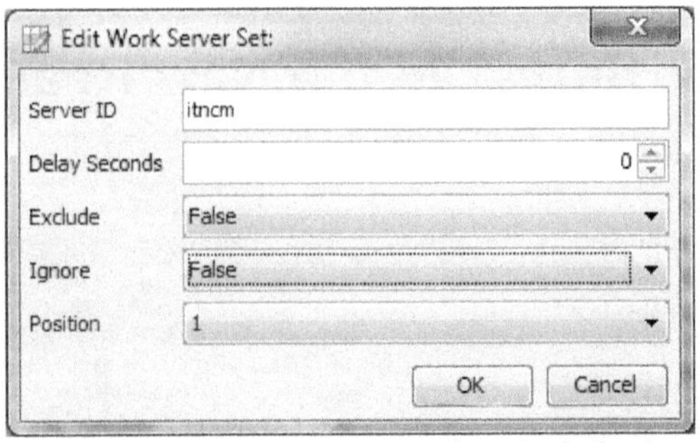

Fill out the form accordingly. Ensure that Ignore is set to False. It defaults to True. And click OK.

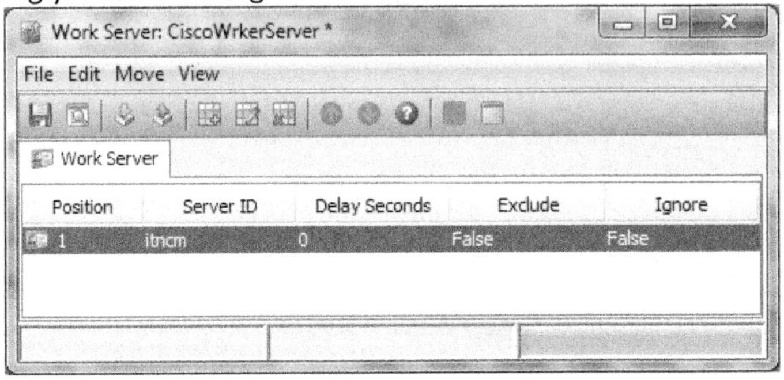

Click the Disk Icon to save the configuration and click File->Close to exit.

Create Authentication in Sub Realm (for Device Passwords)

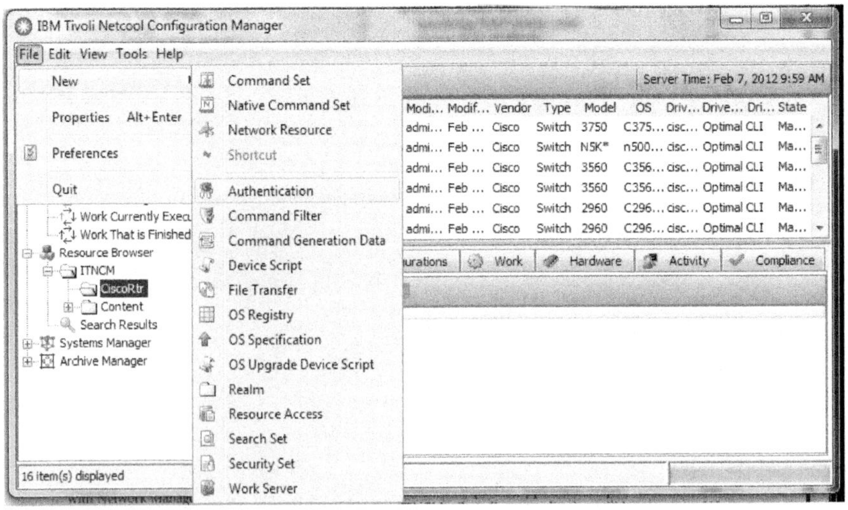

After selecting the ITNCM realm (folder) in the left hand panel, click on File->New->Authentication to create a new set of password keys

Name the authentication and fill out the form and click OK.

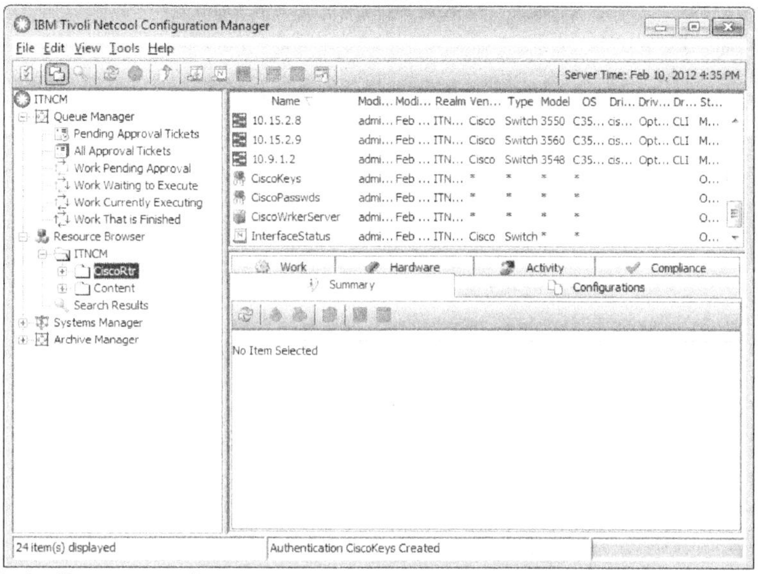

Scroll down and find the "Cisco Keys" entry or whatever the authentication was called and double click on the entry.

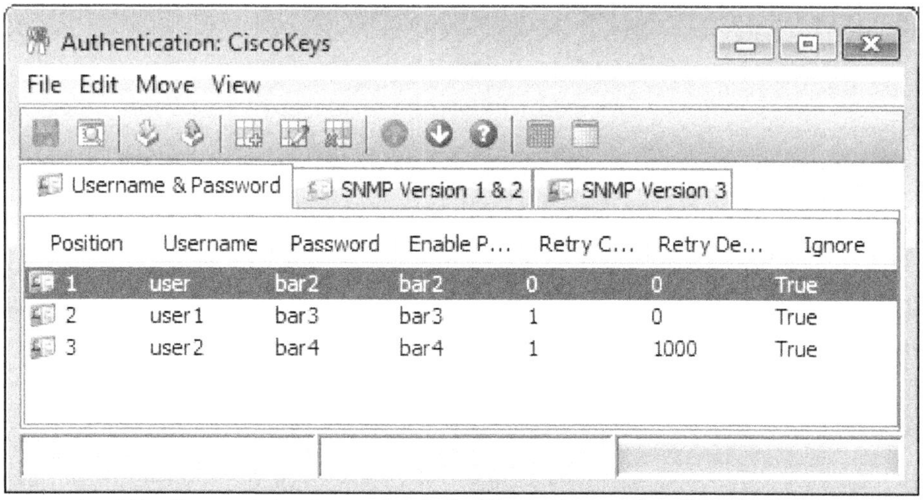

Double click on each of the line entries to correctly indicate the credentials. Make sure to also set Ignore to False (instead of the default True) in order to enable the line.

Add "Normal" Devices via the CLI

This is the best method to add devices. They can be added in bulk via the command line. The first step is to logon as the primary ITNCM user and change directory to the auto discovery folder:

```
su - icosuser
cd /opt/IBM/tivoli/netcool/ncm/autodiscovery/
```

Next, create a file with the user (a), password (p), and enable (e) credentials of the devices to be discovered, specify a directory where the results will be stored (d), specify the realm to hold the devices (r) and finally list the IP addresses and/or host names of the devices to discover:

```
vi company.txt     # OPEN A NEW FILE
a:RtrCredential
p:RtrCredential
e:RtrCredential
d:./results
r:ITNCM/CiscoRtr
10.15.2.9
:::  << ADD MORE IP ADDRESSES TO BE DISCOVERED >> :::
10.15.2.125
```

Next, run the program to discover the devices:

```
./autodiscover.sh company.txt
```

Once complete the results will be stored in the folder specified. Navigate to the directory and look at the date timestamped files.

```
cd results
ls
  20120207102111-AutoDiscovery_log.txt
  20120207102111-BulkLoad.csv
  20120207102111-ConnectionScan.csv
  20120207102111-LoginResults.txt
```

The successfully parsed devices can be loaded into ITNCM using the following command:

```
/opt/IBM/tivoli/netcool/ncm/bin/icosutil  BulkLoader -l administrator -
      p administrator -update -f 20120207102111-BulkLoad.csv
```

Add a "Normal" Device via GUI

Introduction

This is the second best method to add devices. Since they have to be manually entered, this can be cumbersome if there are large number of devices. In this case there were a handful so the CLI method is not required. All but 6 devices were entered successfully using this method.

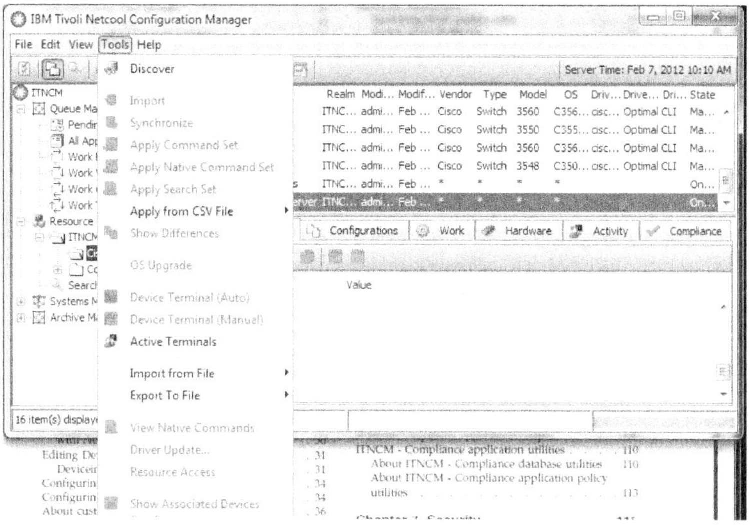

To add a device via the GUI first navigate to the newly created Sub Realm (i.e. CiscoRtr folder)
Next, select the menu option: Tools->Discover

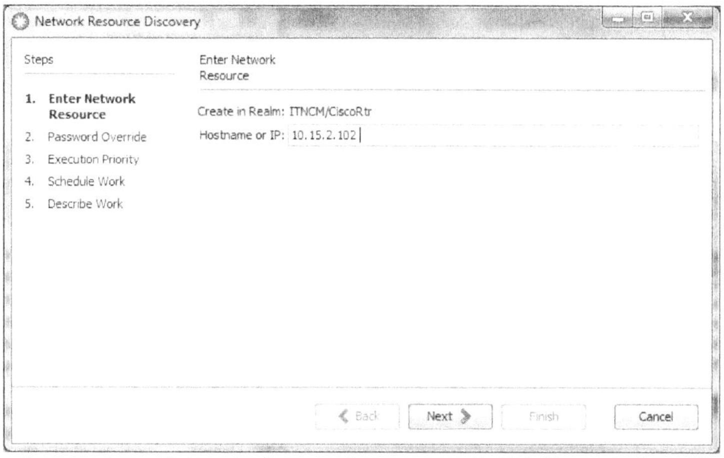

Enter the IP address or hostname of the device to discover and click Next 4x (to skip the windows: Password Override, Execution Priority, Schedule Work)

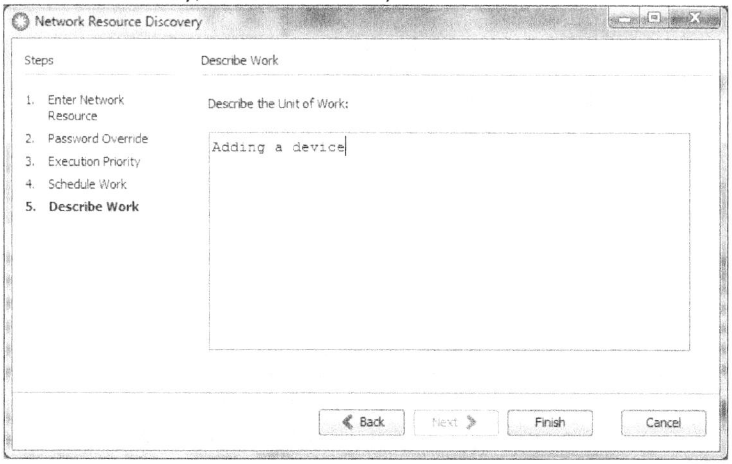

In the final window enter some descriptive text to enable the Finish button and click Finish.

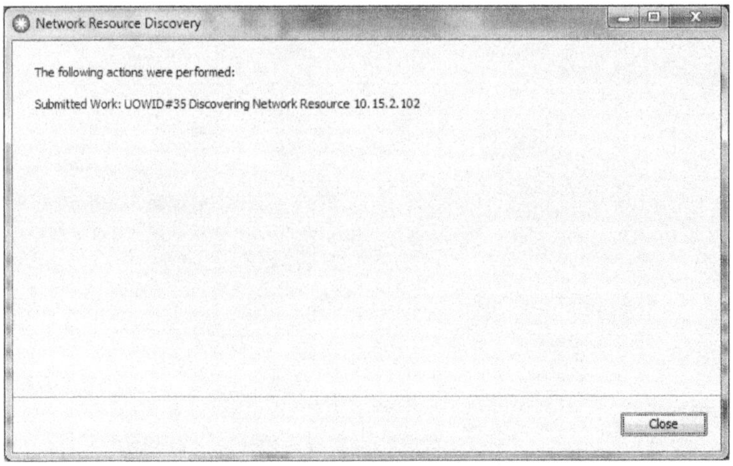

Click close

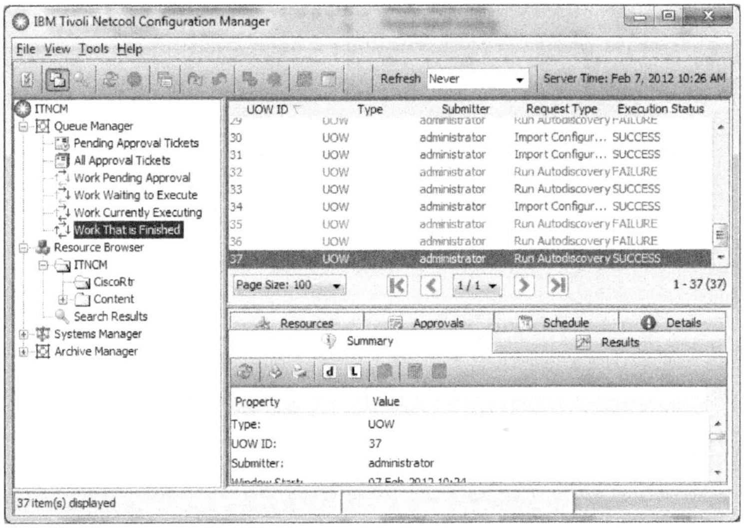

Navigate to Work That is Finished and verify the discovery worked.

Add a "difficult" Device via GUI

Not all devices are easy to acquire via ITNCM. This often is due to ITNCM not parsing the output correctly. In particular there were four devices that had trouble:

Host	IP
WS-C2950SX-48-SI	10.15.2.6
WS-C2950SX-48-SI	10.15.2.7
WS-C2950SX-48-SI	10.15.2.5
WS-C3560X-48	10.15.2.35

For these the type of devices had to be manually specified, rather than automatically determined. This was done via the menu by selecting File->New->Network Resource

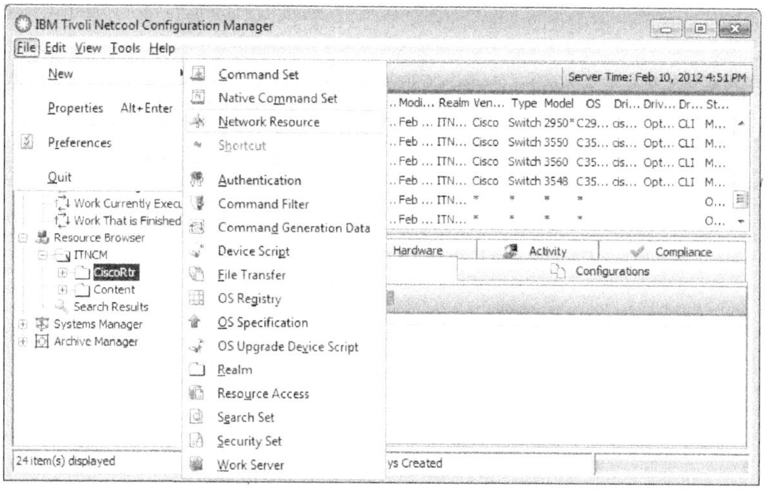

This will open the following form:

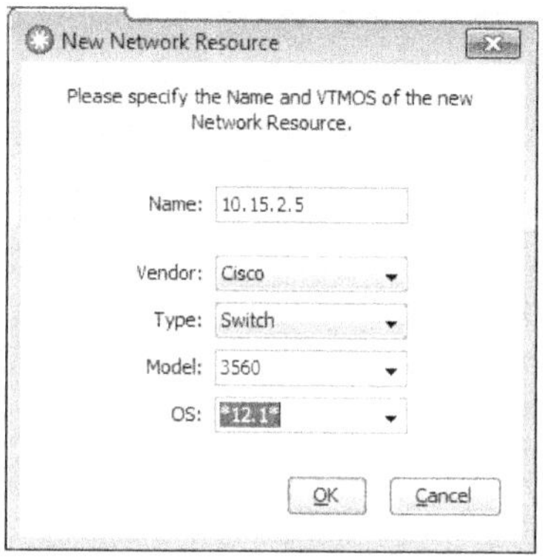

Fill out the form and click OK. A non highlighted version of the device will appear. Right click on the device and select Import.

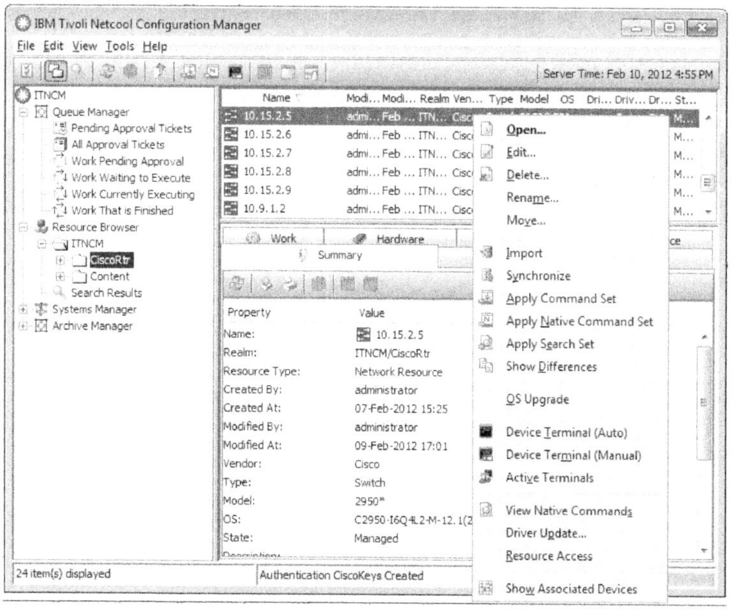

Follow the steps to manually import the device.

Add a "very difficult" Device

Sometimes devices are not supported by ITNCM. In this case, the command line needs to be used to create a registration of the device.

First, stop ITNCM:

```
cd /opt/IBM/tivoli/netcool/ncm/bin
./itncm.sh stop
```

Once stopped, next run the utility and answer the prompts to create a new registration of a device:

```
cd utils
./driverTools.sh -create-standard
      Loading driver information from database...
      Creating content for a standard network resource. Please specify
      the following values...
        Vendor: Cisco
        Type: Switch
        Model: C4506
        OS: 03.01.01.SG
        Display Name (Default: Cisco_Switch_C4506_03.01.01.SG):
        Supported Model(s): C4506
        Supported Os(es): 03*
        Description: Cisco_Switch_C4506_03.01.01.SG

      Please confirm the following details are correct ...
        UUID: Msd1328807997418
        Vendor: Cisco
        Type: Switch
        Model: C4506
        OS: 03.01.01.SG
        Display Name: Cisco_Switch_C4506_03.01.01.SG
        Supported Model(s): C4506
        Supported Os(es):03*
        Description:Cisco_Switch_C4506_03.01.01.SG

      Are these details correct? (Y/N)y
      Successfully created the new standard driver.
      Please restart your server for the changes to take effect.
```

Now when the GUI is accessed and the File->New->Network Resource is accessed the new device type is available:

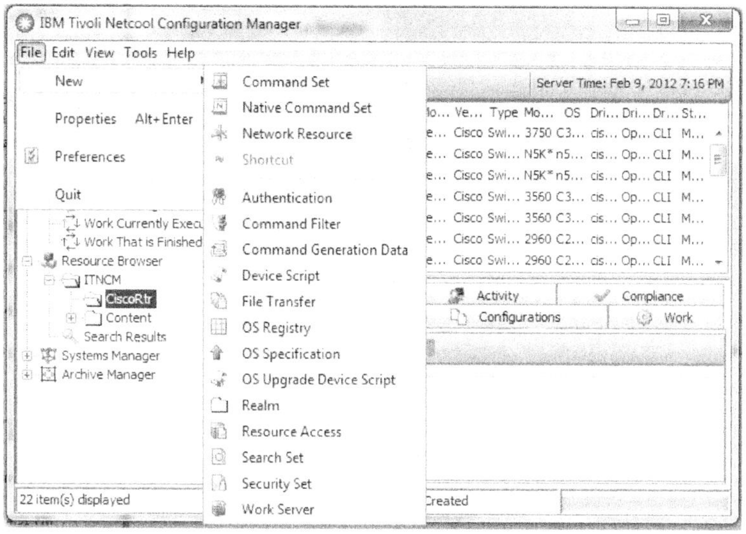

Fill out the form as shown in the previous section:

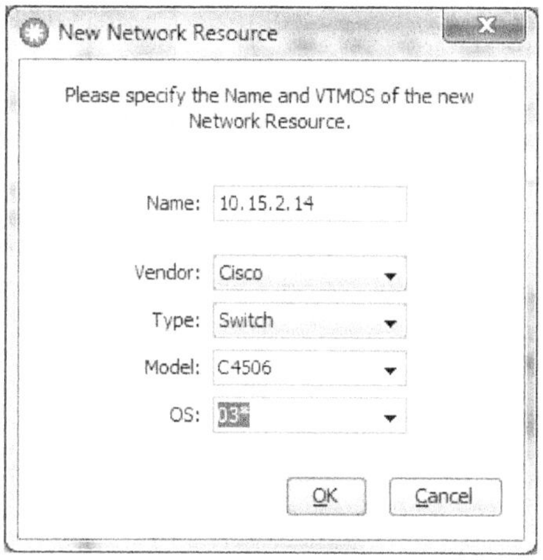

Next, right click on the device and select Resource Access in order to modify how ITNCM interacts with the device:

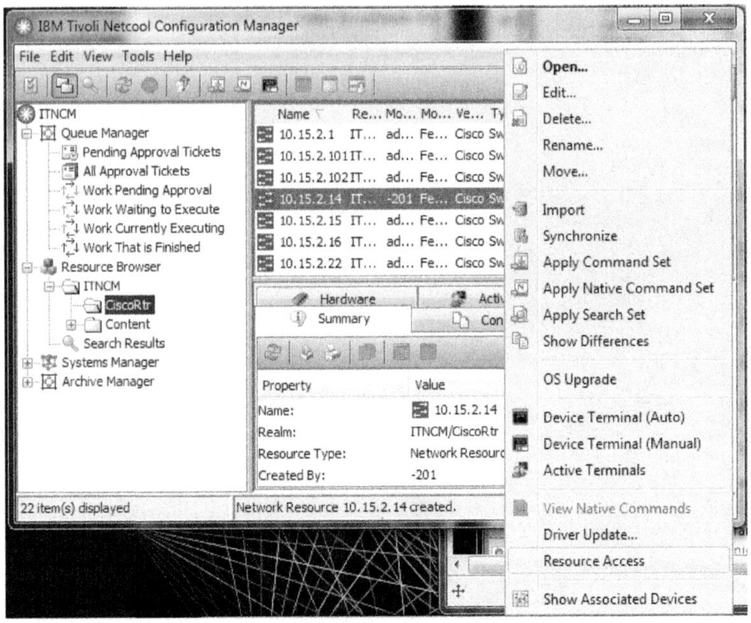

Click Edit on the next screen

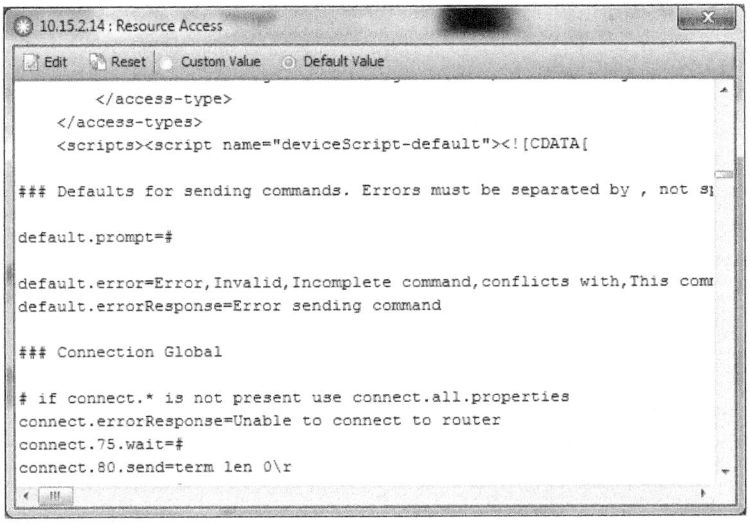

This will bring up the following window. Click on sh, telnet, and alt-telnet in the left hand window. In each case make sure in the right hand window the Enabled check box is UNCHECKED except for telnet which should be CHECKED.

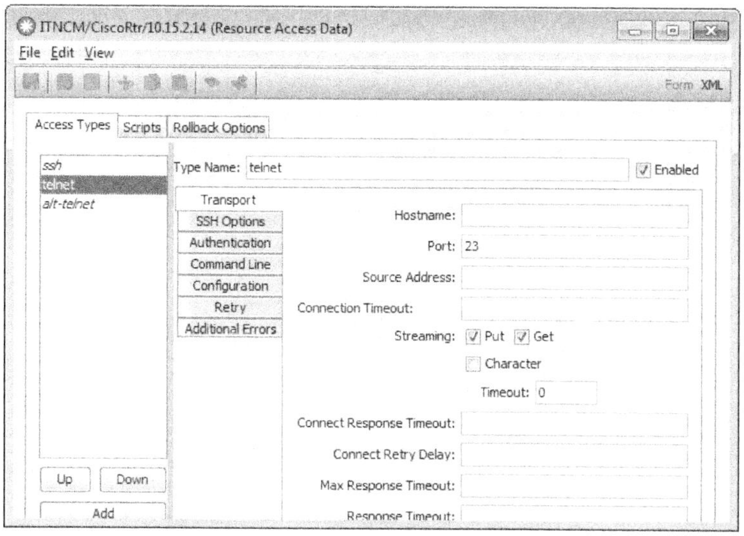

Next, click on Telnet in the left window and then click on the Command Line. For the script field, select "deviceScript-default"

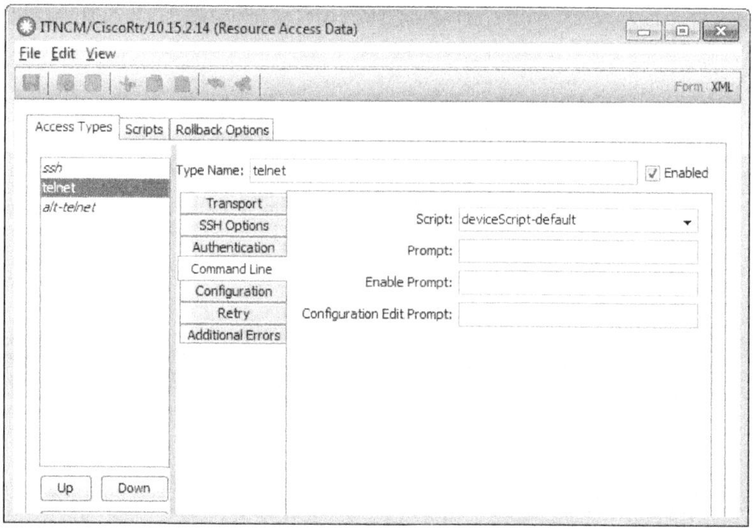

Next, click on the Scripts tab, click on "deviceScript-default" in the left menu and finally scroll down to the connect section and replace it with the following:

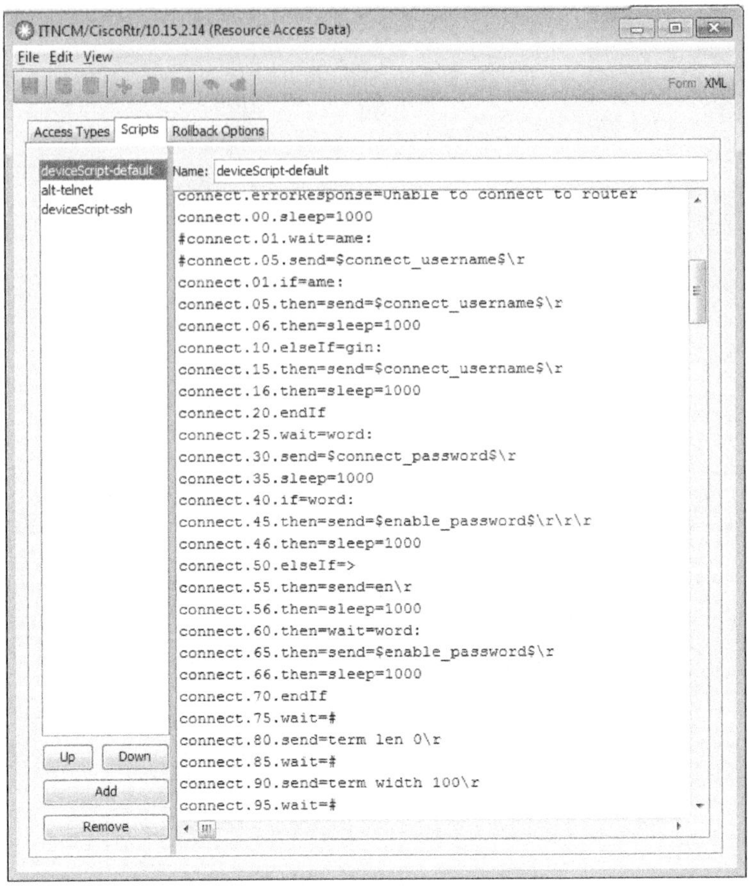

Next, scroll down to the Version section and replace the FIND-END parameter to match what the router uses:

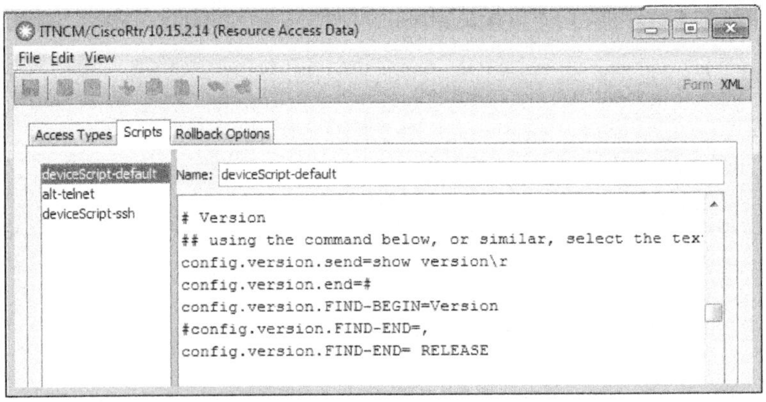

Finally, scroll down to the Copy Running Config to Stored section to correct its parsing:

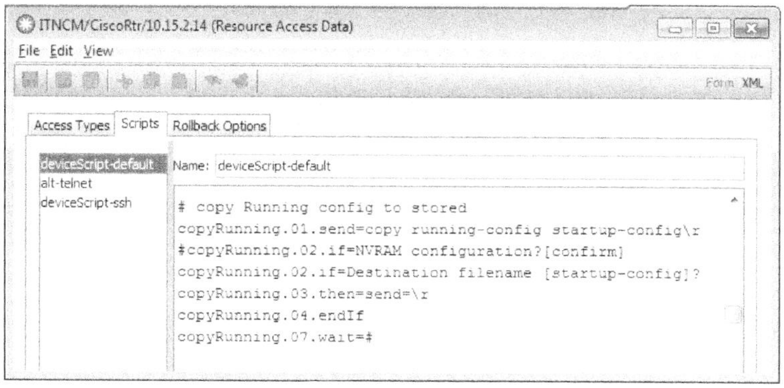

Once the device's interactive script has been corrected, the next step is to import the device:

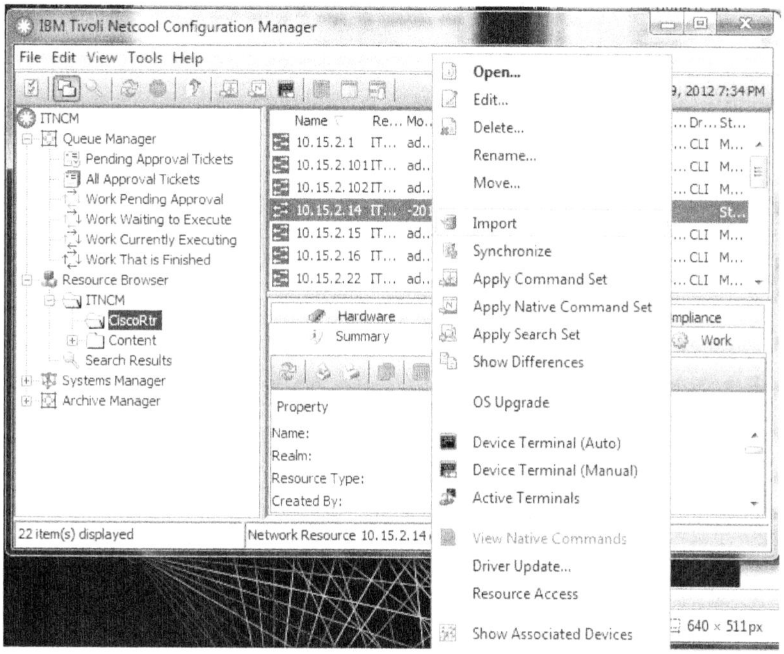

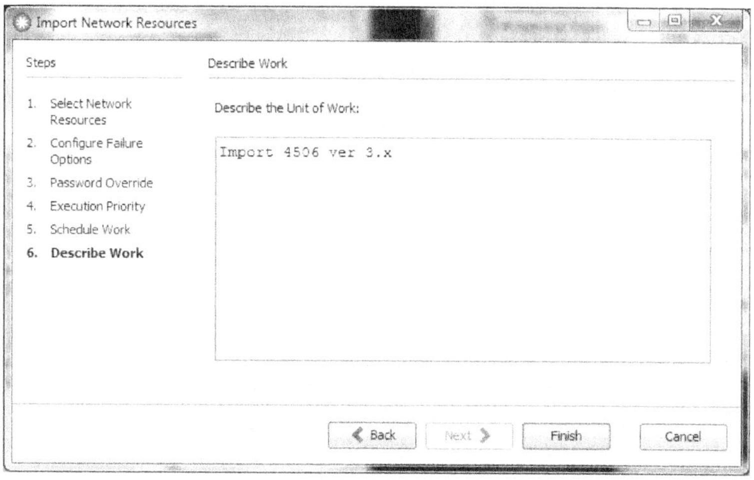

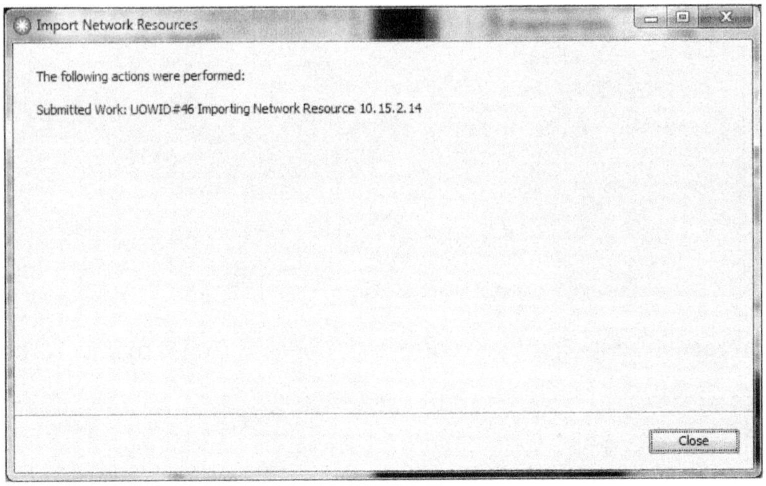

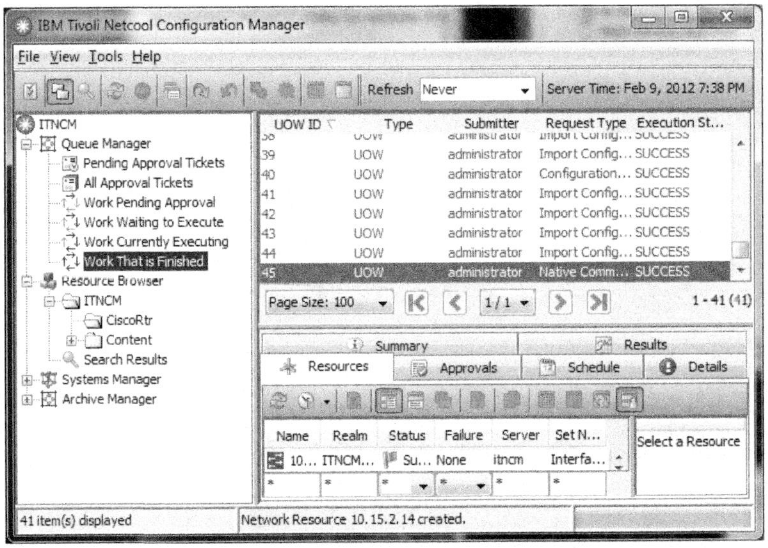

Finally, the device is correctly imported into the ITNCM application.

Create a Native Command Set

Sets of commands can be created and ran across multiple devices. The following is an example of how a native command can be placed into a command set.

A new command set can be created by accessing from the menu: File->New->Command Set

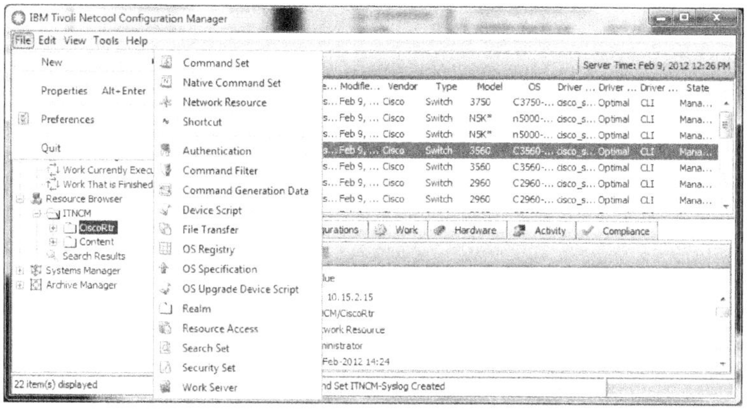

Specify the name of the command set and which devices are affected:

Next, provide the native commands and indicate whether it is a configuration or a interrogation.

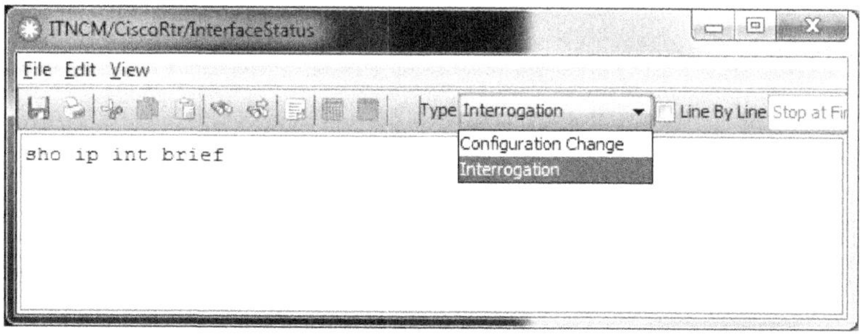

Click the Disk icon to save the command set and click File->Close to exit the window.

Enable Policies in ITNCM Compliance GUI

Thought the policies have been imported due to a lack of permissions, no one will be able to see them. The following steps adds rights for the Administrator group so that the administrator user will be able to see the policies. First login as administrator/administrator and get the following screen

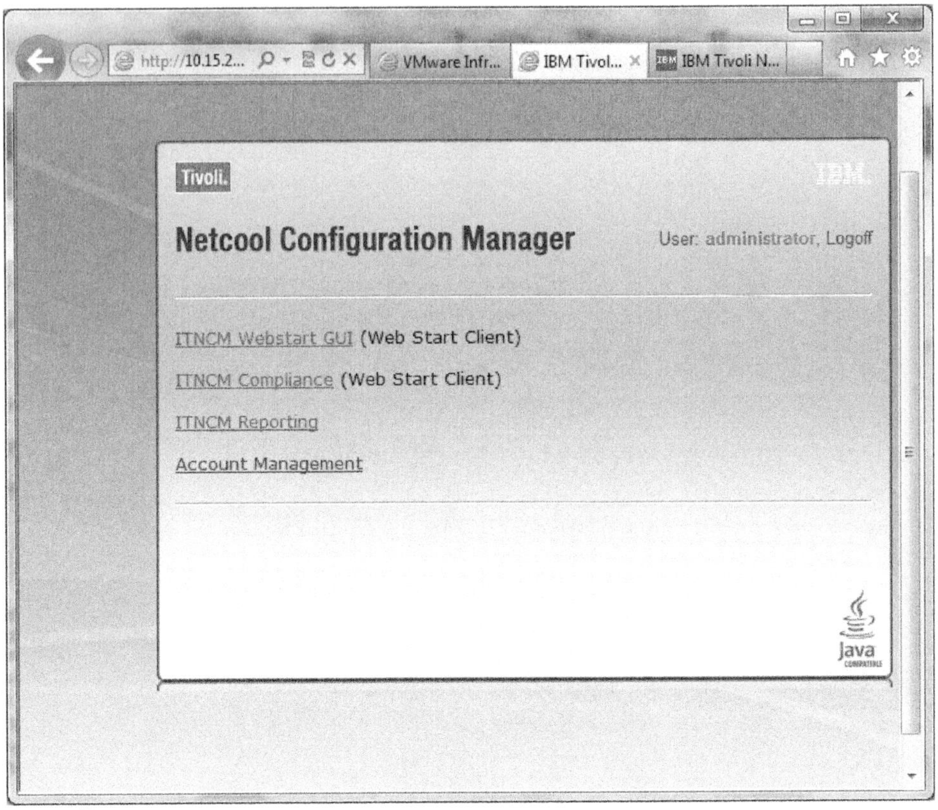

Click ITNCM Compliance

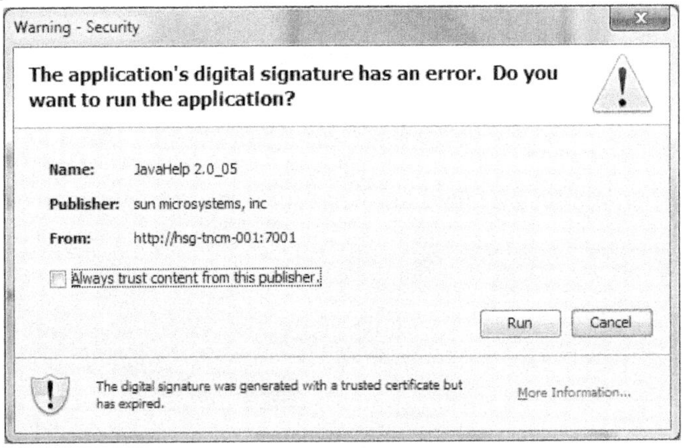

Click the check box and RUN. Once the Compliance manager GUI appears, select from the top menu Admin->User Security Option

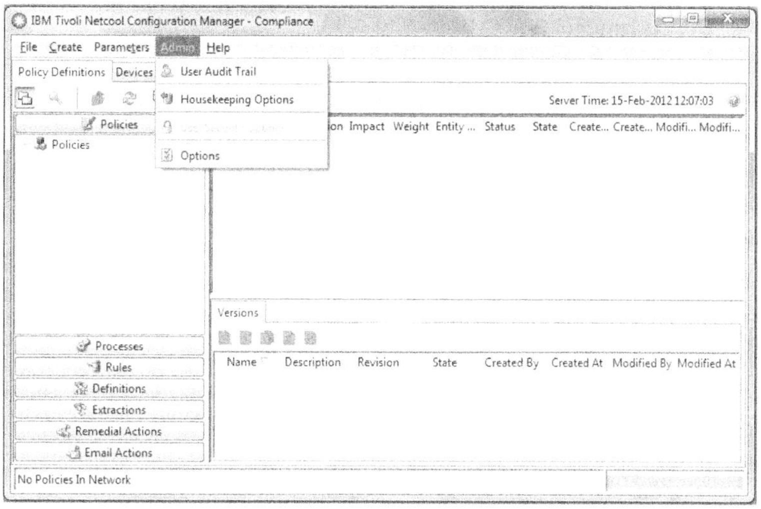

This will change the window to the following. Select Misc Policies and click Add Group(s) button

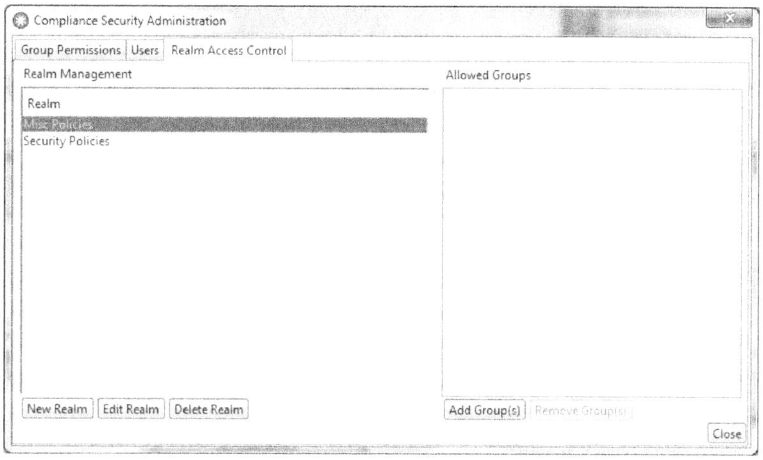

Select Administrator and click Add.

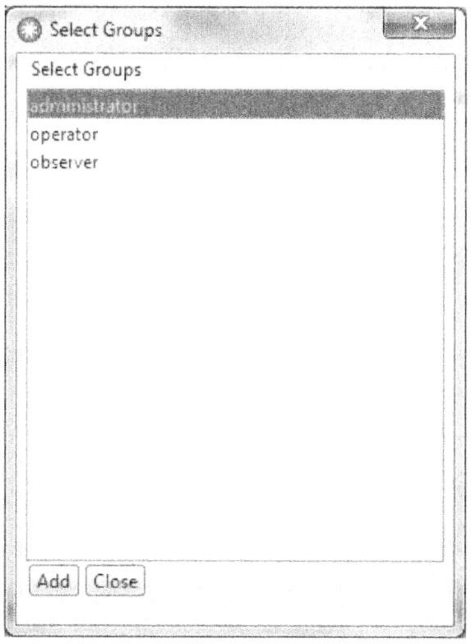

Next click on Security Policies and click Add Group(s) and repeat the process above to add the administrator group.

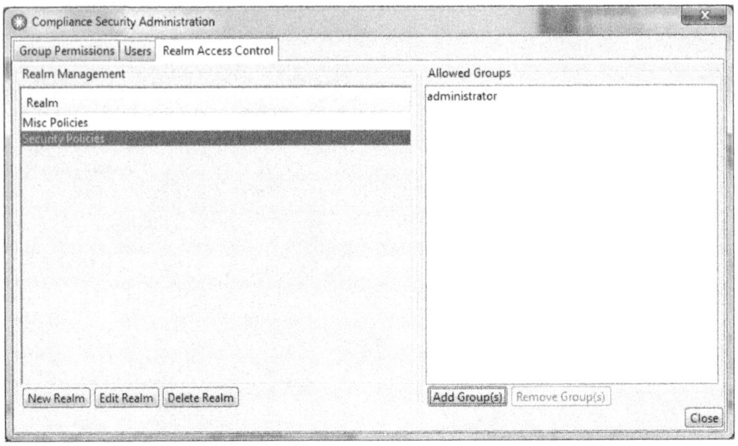

Now click close. The policies will not immediately appear. First close the Compliance GUI and log back in. Then the following will be seen:

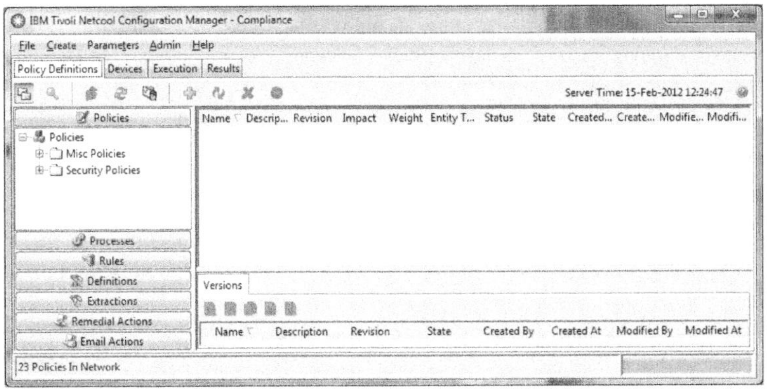

Create New User

In order to customize the authorization and authentication several users and groups were created through the Account Management link.

NOTE: in order to enable Policies and work to be done in ITNCM Compliance additional assignment of policies to groups must be done in the ITNCM Compliance link. For now we will focus on the configuration through the Account Management link.

NOTE: In addition the users need to be added to TCR/TIP to access the reporting functions. This is described in the TCR section. Remember the username and password used here for ITNCM as both need to be added identically to TCR/TIP.

The following users were created:

User Name	Group	Password	Description
David.Needles	ALL	ITNCM	Administration permissions everywhere.
Phillip.Key	Observer	ITNCM	Observer permissions everywhere.
Billy.George	operatorSwitch	ITNCM	Operator permissions in the folder (realm) CiscoSwitches, observer permissions everywhere else.
Rick.Pieklo	operatorSwitch	ITNCM	Operator permissions in the folder (realm) CiscoSwitches, observer permissions everywhere else.
Chris.Sanders	operatorSwitch	ITNCM	Operator permissions in the folder (realm) CiscoSwitches, observer permissions everywhere else.

NOTE: The operatorSwitch is a custom Group and its creation is described later in this document.

Now login as administrator/administrator and get the following screen

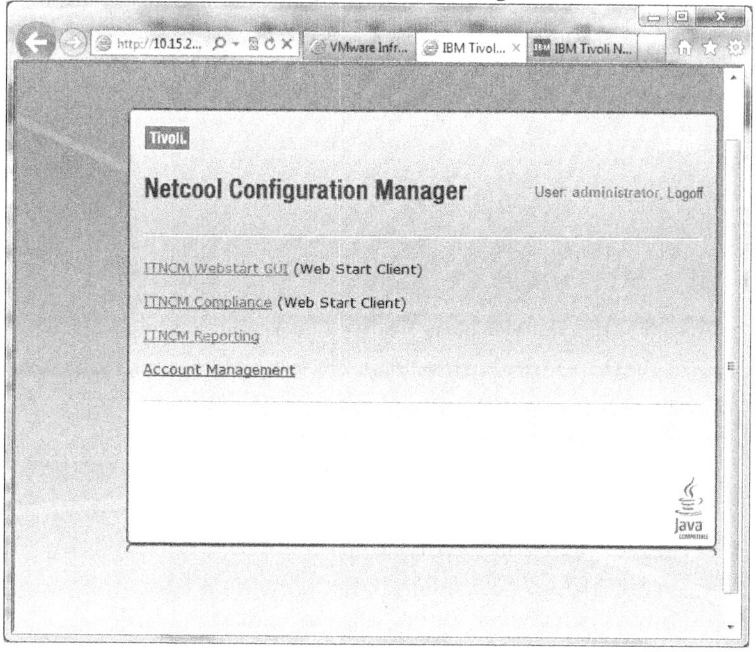

Click Account Management

This will bring you to the Account Management web page:

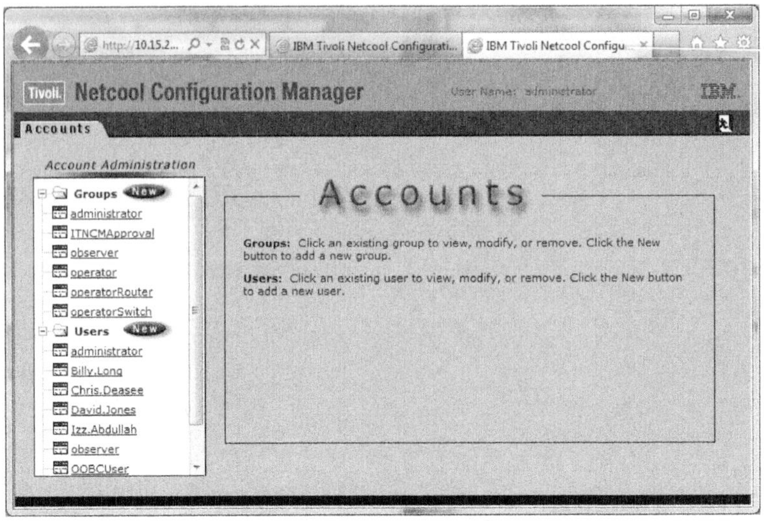

To create a new user, click the "New" button to the right of Users in the left-hand window and fill out the form. In this case we created Philip.Key and set his Initial password as ITNCM. (This was the initial password used for all users.) Next click the Groups tab in the main windowpane. In this case select the "observer" group and click the right arrow to apply it to Philip. Next in the main windowpane scroll down and right and click Save.

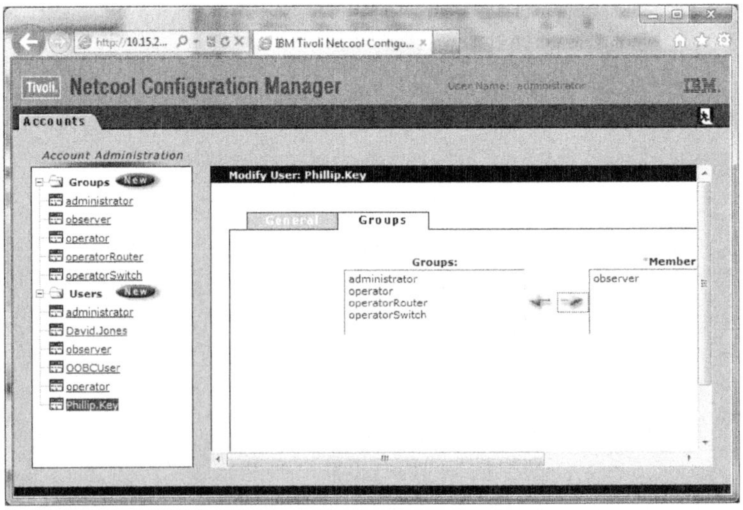

Create Groups

"Switch Operator" group

The group is called OperatorSwitch so that it will group all the Operators together alphabetically. Unfortunately there is no "copy group" equivalent to simplify the process by starting with the operator and modifying. As a result, you first must record the values of the operator group:

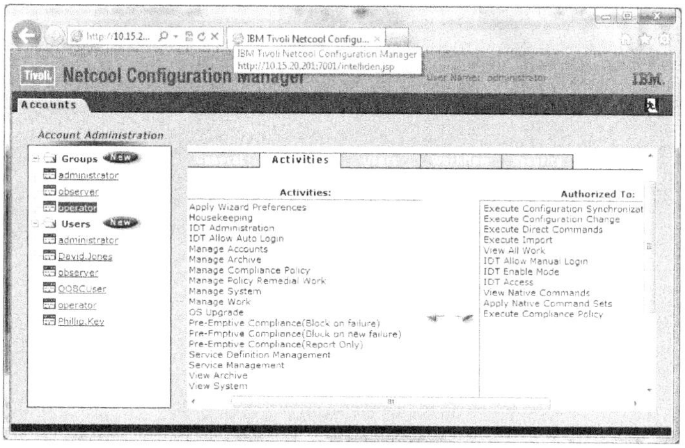

Next, create the group by clicking the "New" button next to groups and filling out the tabs:

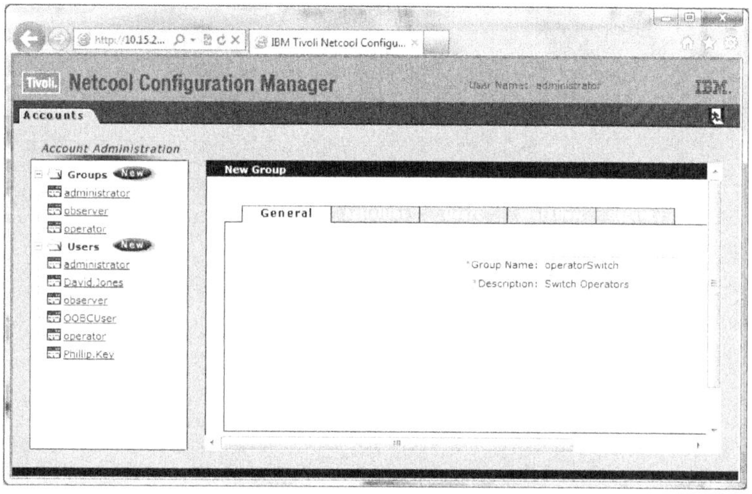

Next, pick the activities to mirror an operator.

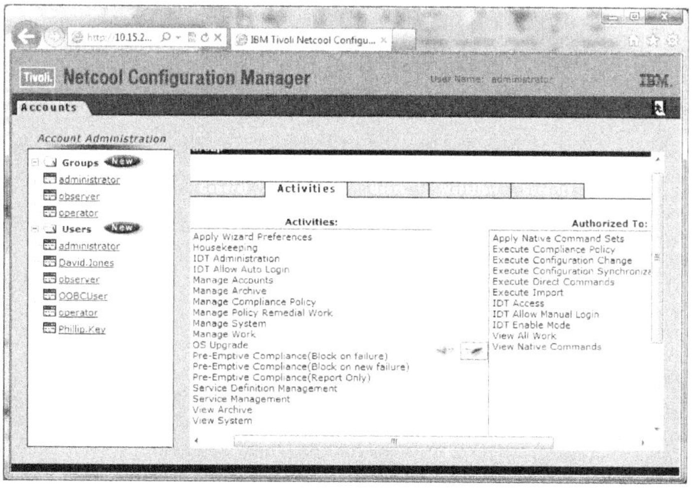

Pick a user for the Group. (Note in this case the other users weren't created yet and thus not selected.)

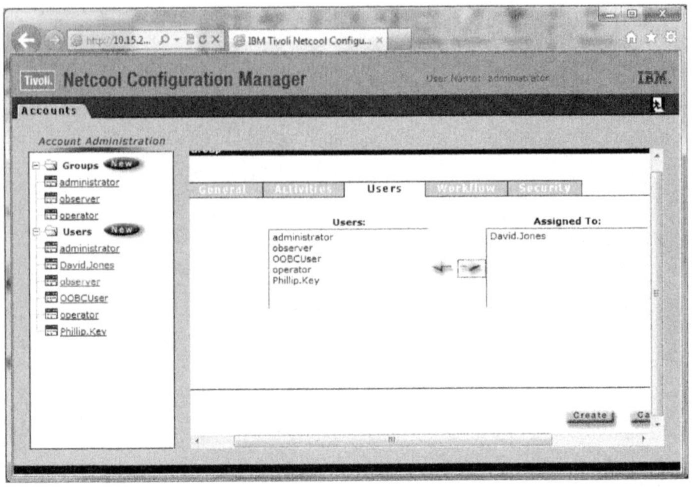

Next, make sure to select Policy Set 1. This means 1 other person needs to authorize any changes by people that belong to this group. Another user has the "Manage" activity under the Activities tab, which enables them to approve or disapprove of changes.

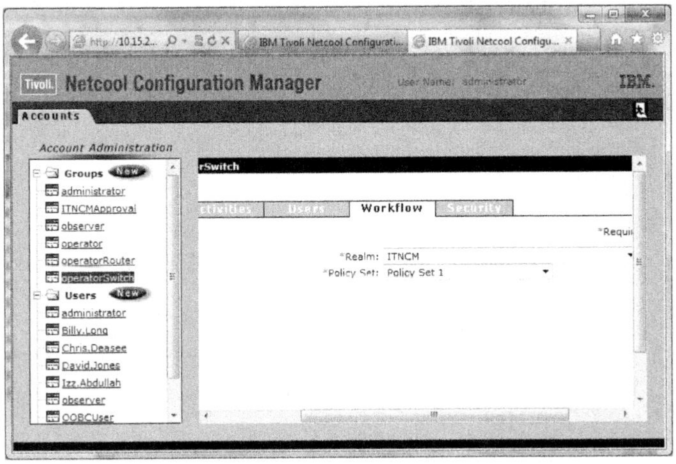

Next, select Security tab and select the first sub tab: Realm. This defines what the users can do to the Realm (i.e. Folders)

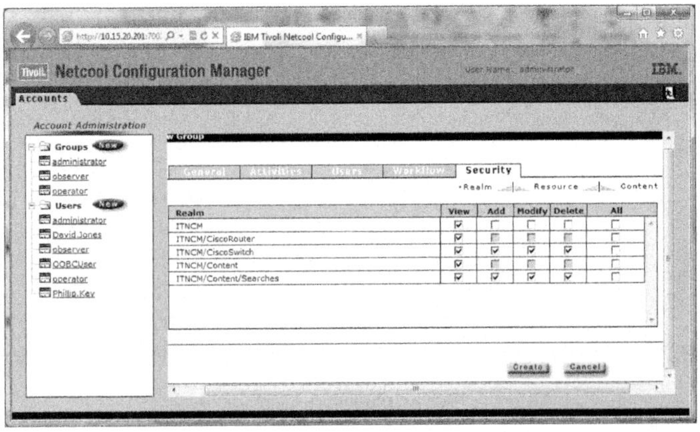

NOTE: Make sure to also get Resources as well as Realms by clicking the Resource sub menu under the Security tab.

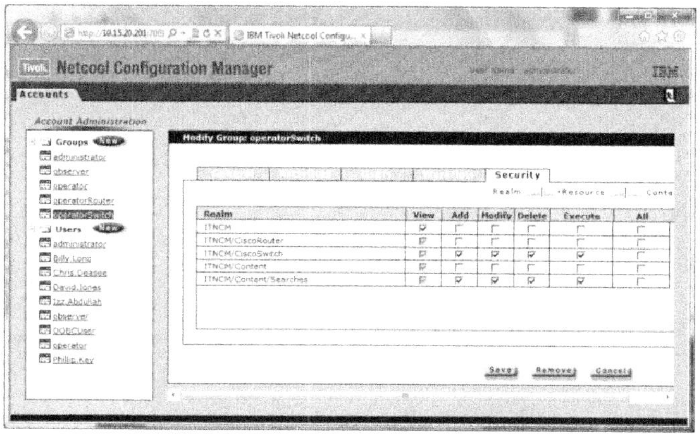

"Router Operator" group

Repeat the identical steps for operatorRouter but instead of providing all Realm permissions to ITNCM/CiscoSwitch, provide those permissions to ITNCM/CiscoRouter.

"ITNCM Approver" group

This group is used specifically to Approve and Disapprove changes. Repeat the identical steps for operatorRouter but instead:

The only Activity is "Manage Work":

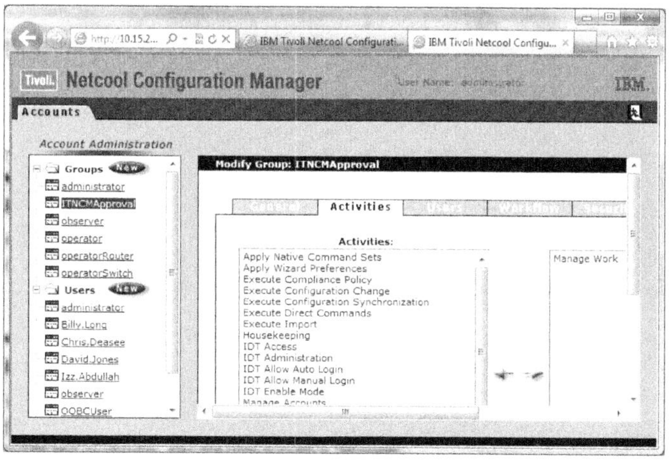

Also the workflow is set so that the Realm "ITNCM" is set and Policy Set 0 is used so that no approvals are needed for these users.

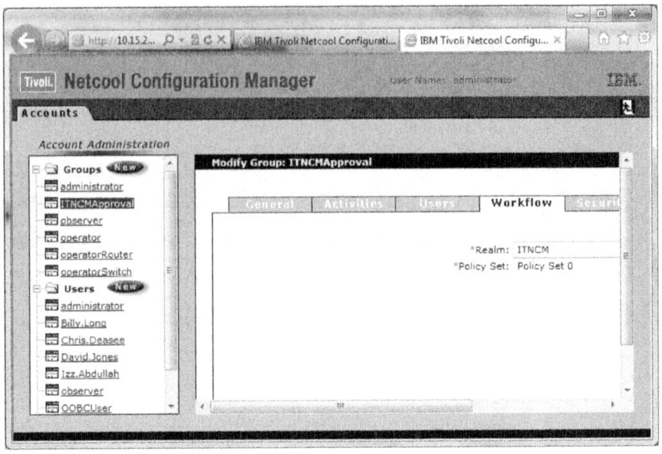

Finally, security is wide open for this group as they can touch all Realms and all Resources.

Create Parameterized Command Set

If you needed to create a SNMP configuration script that allowed you to enter parameters, this is done through a Native Command Set.

First, in the ITNCM Web GUI interface, go to File->New->Native Command Set

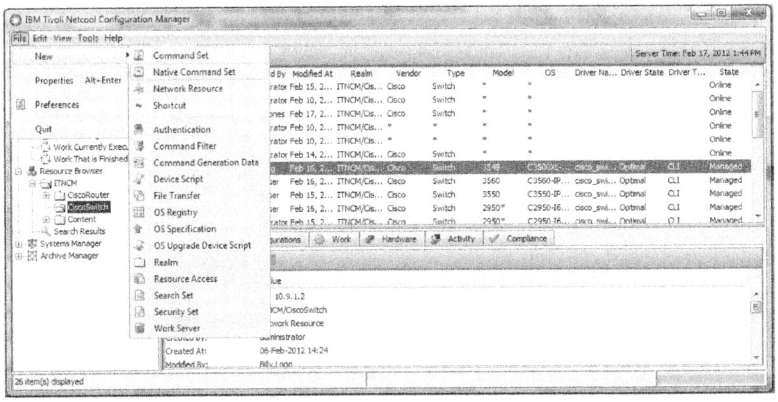

Then fill out the form and click the OK button to create the command set

Once back at the main screen, right click on the newly created command set and select Edit.

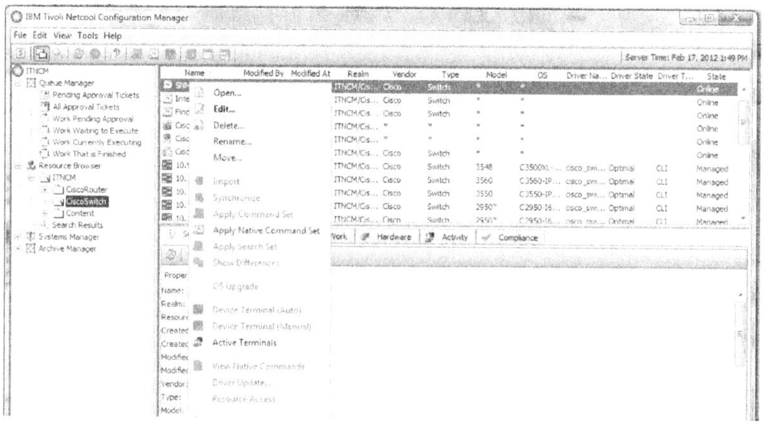

This will open a new window in which you put your native commands.

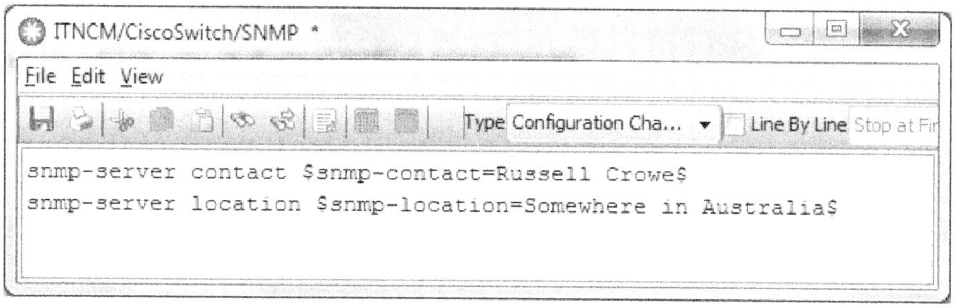

Variables and their default values are delimited by = and the start and finish is delimited by '$'

Click the disk icon to save the command set.

Now the when the Native Command Set is Applied to Devices either from the Command Set or from selected Device(s)

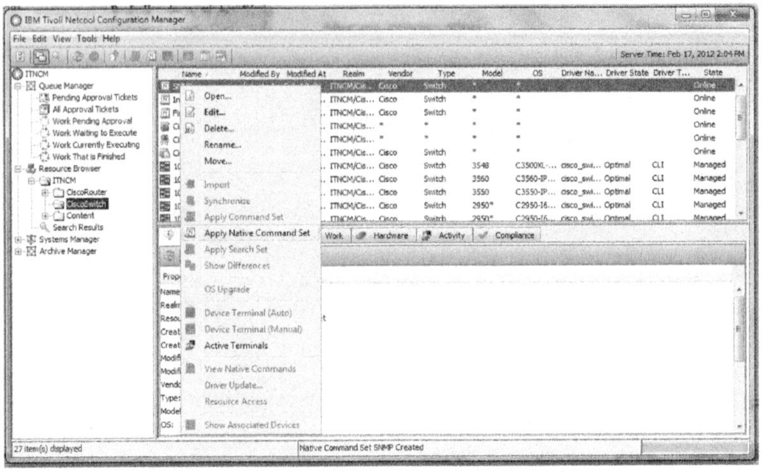

...the Parameter Page will appear:

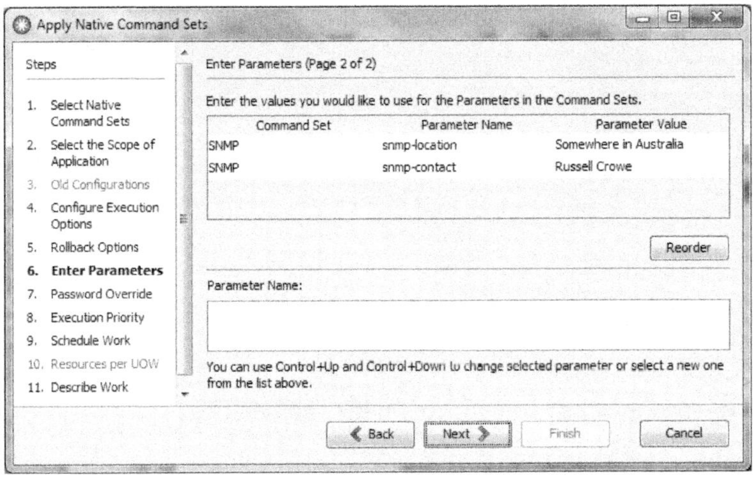

TCR Configuration

The Reporting of ITNCM is common across all Tivoli Netcool products and uses a web portal called TIP. As a result TCR requires additional configuration in order to integrate TCR into ITNCM. Specifically additional configuration for each user is required. This section describes how this is done.

The users to be configured are:

User Name	Group	Password	Description
administrator	ALL	administrator	This is the default Admin user for ITNCM.
David.Needles	ALL	ITNCM	Administration permissions everywhere.
Phillip.Key	Observer	ITNCM	Observer permissions everywhere.
Billy.George	operatorSwitch	ITNCM	Operator permissions in the folder (realm) CiscoSwitches, observer permissions everywhere else.
Rick.Pieklo	operatorSwitch	ITNCM	Operator permissions in the folder (realm) CiscoSwitches, observer permissions everywhere else.
Chris.Sanders	operatorSwitch	ITNCM	Operator permissions in the folder (realm) CiscoSwitches, observer permissions everywhere else.

NOTE: The following default users were NOT configured in TCR/TIP

User Name	Group	Password	Description
operator	N/A	operator	This is the default operator user for ITNCM. They perform the day to day maintenance tasks with the managed devices.
observer	N/A	observer	This is the default observer user for ITNCM. They report and audit the day to day maintenance tasks with the managed devices.

The following are the steps to set up the users in TCR/TIP

1. Start the NCM Server as normal (itncm.sh start). This should also start the TCR Server.
2. On your browser navigate to the following url:
   http://server:16310/ibm/console

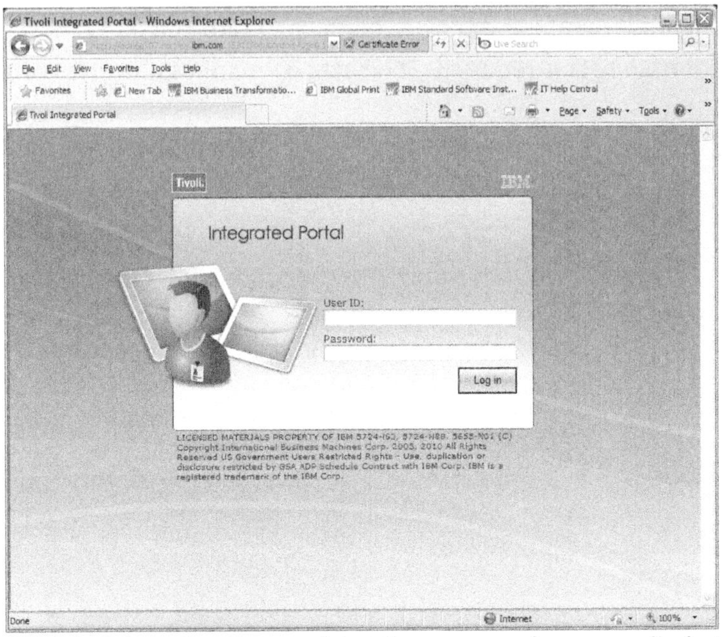

3. Log in as the TIP Administration User and use the password you supplied at install time.

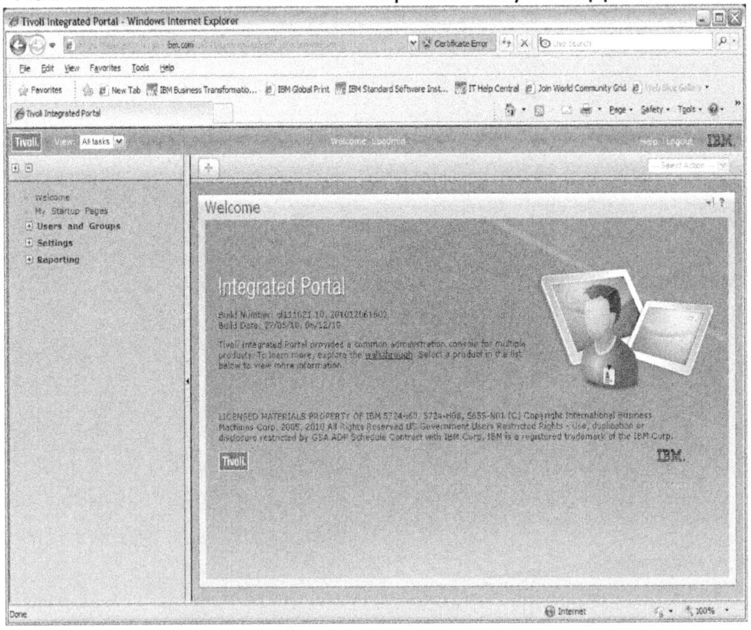

4. Expand Users and Groups and click on Manage Users

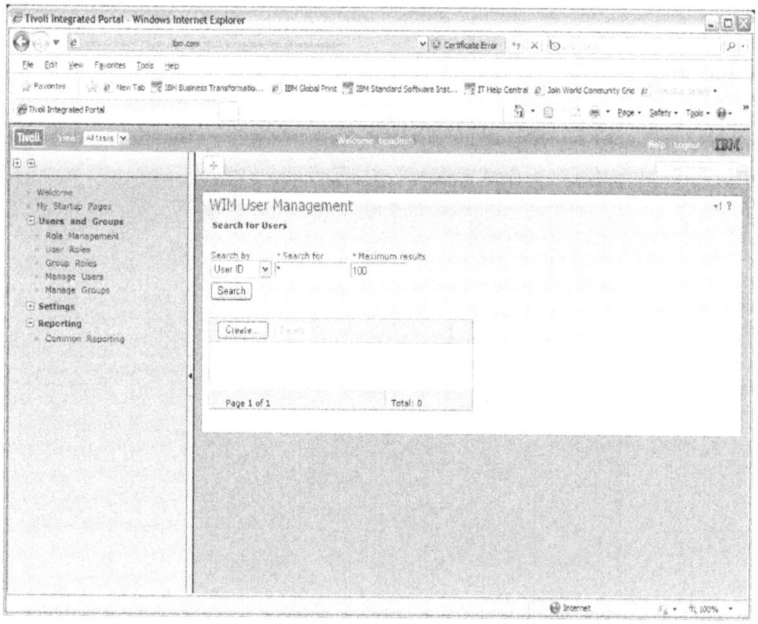

Create a user that matches a user in NCM (administrator for example)

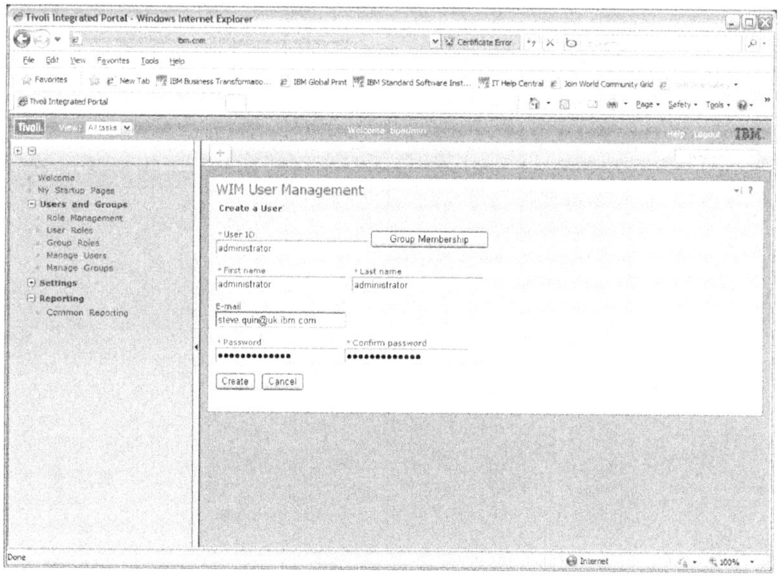

5. Give the user the tcrPortalOperator role. Click on User Roles link and hit search. The user you created will be displayed. Click on that user.

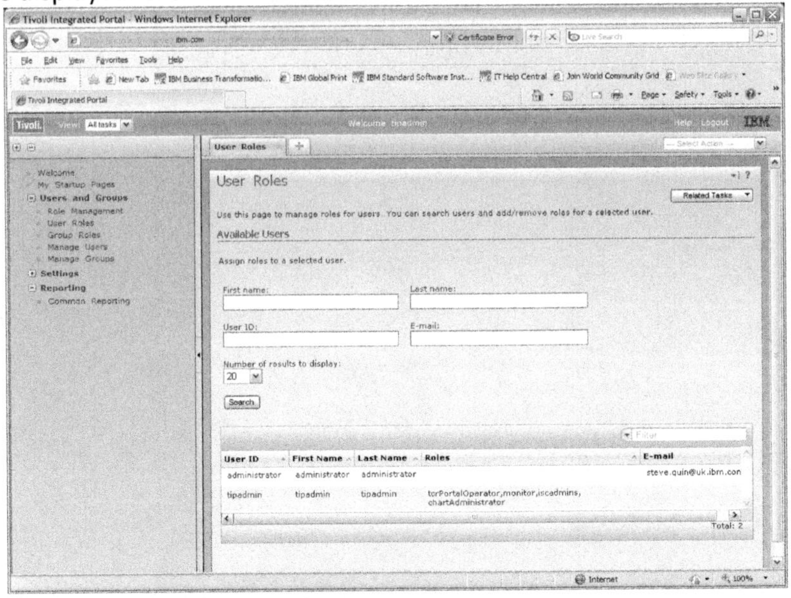

1. Give the user the tcrPortalOperator role and hit save.

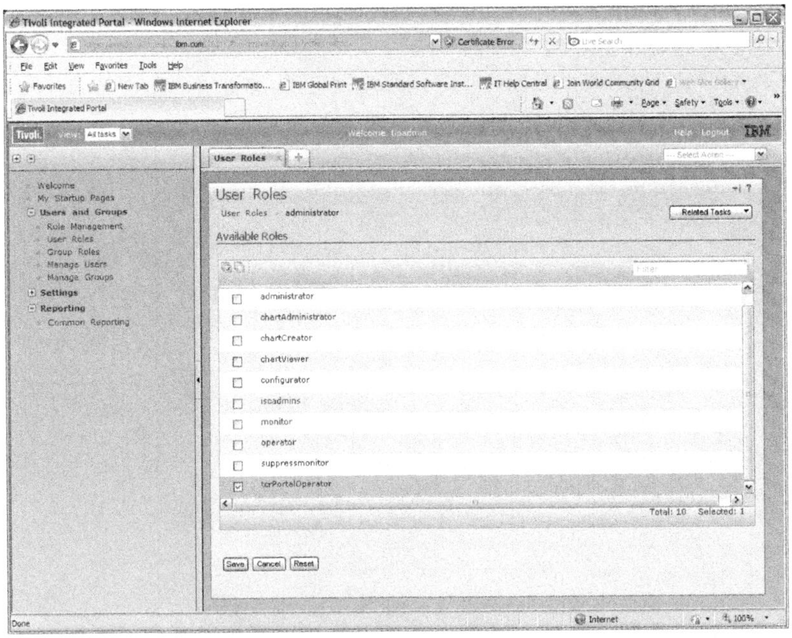

6. Log out of TIP and back in as the user you have just created.

7. Expand Reporting and click on the Common Reporting link

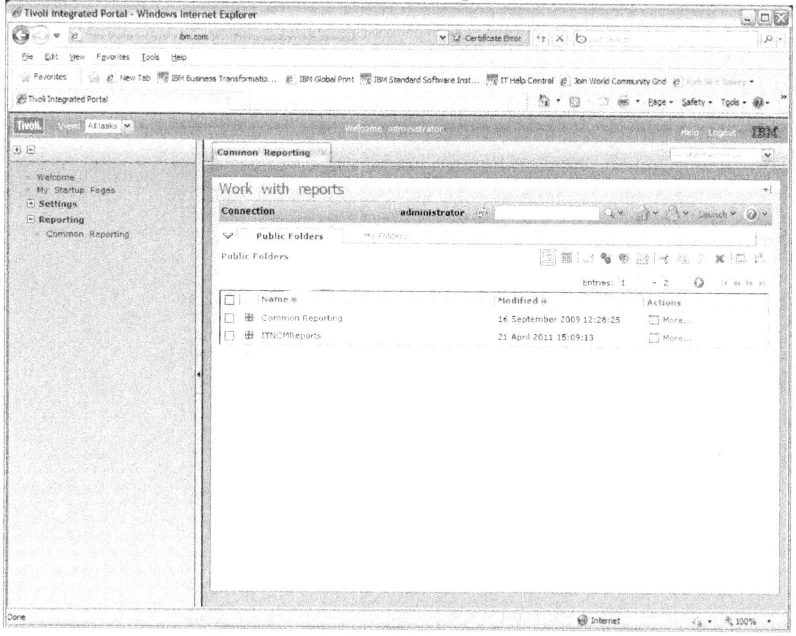

Click on ITNCMReports and you will be given a list of the NCM Reports.

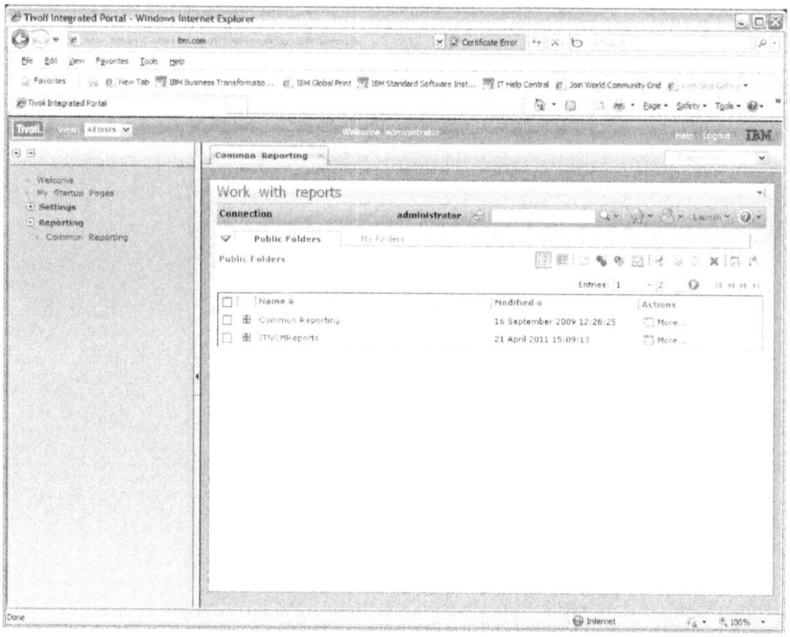

8. Click on a Report to enter the Report criteria

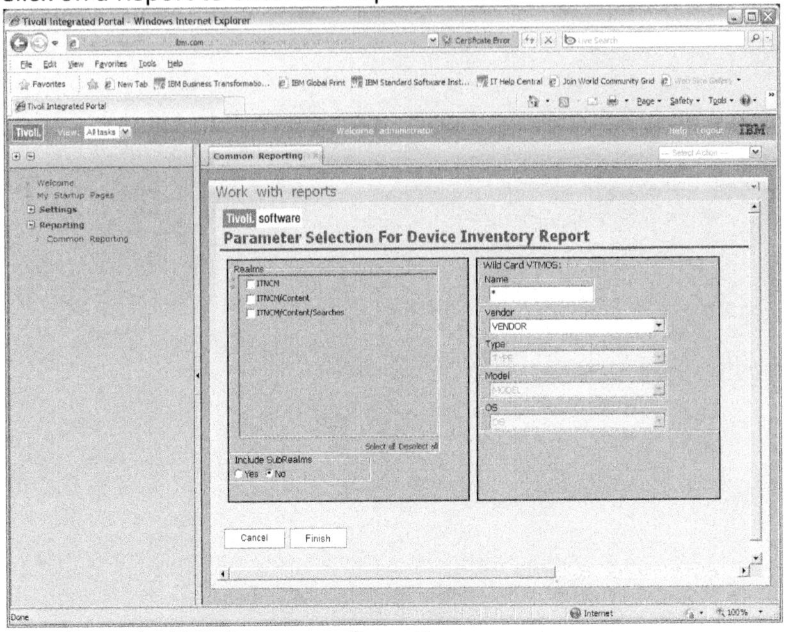

This completes the TCR Report configuration.

ITNCM OOBC Installation (Optional - Out of Band Control)

Introduction

How does ITNCM get alerted when changes are made outside the application? This is the purpose of Out of Band Control (OOBC) Specifically the router, switch or other device is set up to log messages to the ITNCM syslog. Then the OOBC will watch the log for messages it cares about. Any detected changes on the router, switch or other device under ITNCM control triggers ITNCM to go out and pull the configuration. In this way it can keep track of changes on the Network that are done outside the tool. OOBC is configured in the following steps:

- Installation of OOBC
- Update syslog

Installation of OOBC

The following steps were used to install OOBC. First unbundle the OOBC

```
su - icosuser
cd /home/icosuser/TNCM-Install/BASE
mkdir ../OOBC
cp -p oobc.zip ../OOBC/
cd ../OOBC/
unzip oobc.zip
cd OutOfBandChange/
ls
      etc  install  ITNCMBASE0603.SYS2  lib  license
      OOBC_Install_Guide.pdf  tools
```

The installation must be ran as root and the OOBC software was moved to ensure some of the installation defaults could be used to minimize the chance of problems/bugs:

```
su -
Password:
cd /home/icosuser/TNCM-Install/OOBC/OutOfBandChange/install
mkdir -p /opt/oobc
mv OutOfBandChange/ opt/oobc
cd /opt/oobc/OutOfBandChange/install
```

Next, the product was installed

```
./install.sh
      International Program License Agreement

      Part 1 - General Terms

      BY DOWNLOADING, INSTALLING, COPYING, ACCESSING, CLICKING ON
      AN "ACCEPT" BUTTON, OR OTHERWISE USING THE PROGRAM,
```

```
LICENSEE AGREES TO THE TERMS OF THIS AGREEMENT. IF YOU ARE
ACCEPTING THESE TERMS ON BEHALF OF LICENSEE, YOU REPRESENT
AND WARRANT THAT YOU HAVE FULL AUTHORITY TO BIND LICENSEE
TO THESE TERMS. IF YOU DO NOT AGREE TO THESE TERMS,

- DO NOT DOWNLOAD, INSTALL, COPY, ACCESS, CLICK ON AN
"ACCEPT" BUTTON, OR USE THE PROGRAM; AND

- PROMPTLY RETURN THE UNUSED MEDIA, DOCUMENTATION, AND
PROOF OF ENTITLEMENT TO THE PARTY FROM WHOM IT WAS OBTAINED

Press Enter to continue viewing the license agreement, or
enter "1" to accept the agreement, "2" to decline it, "3"
to print it, or "99" to go back to the previous screen.
1
            Beginning install process for new
            OOBC Run directory: /opt/oobc/OutOfBandChange/run1


Enter the Unix owner of the OOBC software? [icosuser:icosgrp]

Enter the server name of ITNCM? [intelliden]
WebGUI-TIP-Server
Is ITNCM running a secure connection (https)? [no]

What port is ITNCM running on [7001]?

What user do you want to login to ITNCM as [OOBCUser]?

Enter clear text password:
PASSWORD
Enter the worker user id ITNCM executes work as [intelliden]?

Enter the worker server address [intelliden]?
WebGUI-TIP-Server
Enter an authorized 3rd party user id that does not require
notification when activity is recorded in the syslog
[3rdPartyUser]?

Enter the full path to the syslog file to be parsed:
[/opt/oobc/OutOfBandChange/run1/local7.log]

Enter the full path to the syslog saver file:
[/opt/oobc/OutOfBandChange/run1/log.syslog-messages]


 Intelliden OOBC Install Properties:
   Install Owner:                 icosuser:icosgrp
   Install Directory:             /opt/oobc/OutOfBandChange/run1
   Intelliden URL:                iiop://WebGUI-TIP-Server:7001/
   Syslog File:
/opt/oobc/OutOfBandChange/run1/local7.log
   OOBC User:             OOBCUser
   User Password:         456c1f4db11786c2
   Intelliden Worker:     intelliden
   3rd Party User:        3rdPartyUser
   Worker Server:                 WebGUI-TIP-Server
```

```
  Syslog Message Storage File:
/opt/oobc/OutOfBandChange/run1/log.syslog-messages

Is this OK?  (yes, no)
yes
Copying Configuration Files
Setting permissions

Creating symbolic links for Linux
  /etc/rc.d/rc0.d/K87OOBCDaemon_run1
  /etc/rc.d/rc1.d/K87OOBCDaemon_run1
  /etc/rc.d/rc2.d/S13OOBCDaemon_run1
  /etc/rc.d/rc3.d/S13OOBCDaemon_run1
  /etc/rc.d/rc4.d/S13OOBCDaemon_run1
  /etc/rc.d/rc5.d/S13OOBCDaemon_run1
  /etc/rc.d/rc6.d/K87OOBCDaemon_run1


BUILD SUCCESSFUL
Total time: 1 minutes 30 seconds
```

Update Syslog

The next step is to change the Syslog configuration on the ITNCM server. This is done in a series of steps:

Open IP Tables

Reconfigure Syslog Daemon

Open IP Tables

The first step is to alter your iptables/ip6tables rulesets (/etc/sysconfig/{iptables,ip6tables}) to permit traffic on UDP port 514 (this was not needed but placed here in case it comes up):

```
-A RH-Firewall-1-INPUT -s 192.168.10.0/25 -m udp -p udp --dport 514 -j
ACCEPT

-A RH-Firewall-1-INPUT -s fc00::/7 -m udp -p udp --dport 514 -j ACCEPT
```

Change the "-s" parameter to accurately reflect the range of IP addresses you want to accept syslog messages from. The stock syslogd has no authentication so this is basically your only line of defense against random machines sending messages to you.

Next, reload your iptables/ip6tables rules with:

```
/usr/bin/sudo /sbin/service iptables restart
/usr/bin/sudo /sbin/service ip6tables restart
```

Reconfigure Syslog Daemon

First, edit /etc/sysconfig/syslog. Add "-r" to the SYSLOGD_OPTIONS line:

```
SYSLOGD_OPTIONS="-m 0 -r"
```

Next restart syslogd with:

```
/usr/bin/sudo /sbin/service syslog restart
```

(note that the service is 'syslog' and not 'syslogd')

Next, verify that syslogd is listening on port 514 using netstat:

```
sudo netstat -anp | grep 514
      udp        0      0 0.0.0.0:514       0.0.0.0:*        5332/syslogd
```

Update /etc/syslog.conf adding two lines to the end of the file:

```
# ITNCM OOBC Needs to get Messages.
local7.*      /opt/oobc/OutOfBandChange/run1/local7.log
```

Update Managed Routers and Switches

Next, validate configuration and that syslog is getting updated by manually configuring one router or switch:

```
telnet 10.15.2.15
      Trying 10.15.2.15...
      Connected to rtr.company.com (10.15.2.15).
      Escape character is '^]'.


      User Access Verification

      Password:
rtr>en
      Password:
rtr#config t
      Enter configuration commands, one per line.  End with CNTL/Z.
rtr(config)#logging buffered 4096 notifications
rtr(config)#logging WebGUI-TIP-Server
      logging source-interface Vlan 2   (10.15.2.14)
rtr(config)#end
rtr#write mem
      Building configuration...
      [OK]
```

Create OODB User

The actions done within ITNCM on behalf of OODB are done via a user. The installation does not automatically create this user - so it must be done manually. The first step is to navigate to the Netcool Configuration Manager. Once there you enter the user's information, using the username and password specified in the installer.

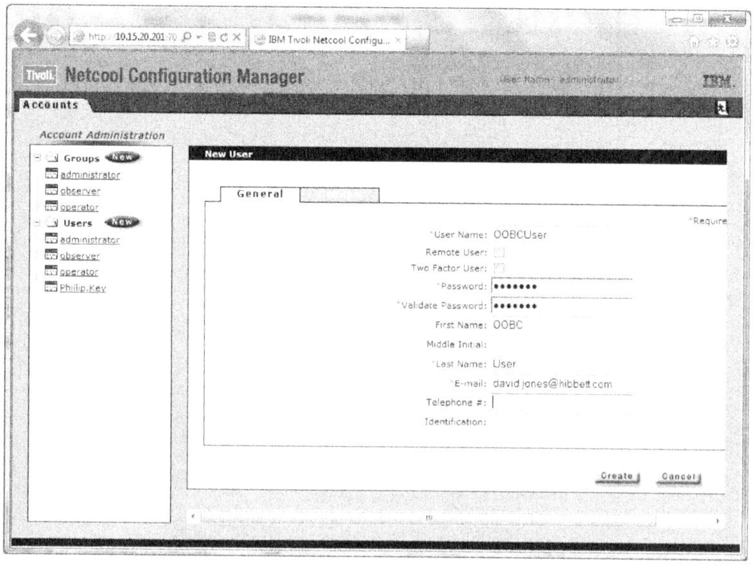

Next you specify that the user belong to the Administrator group and click the create button.

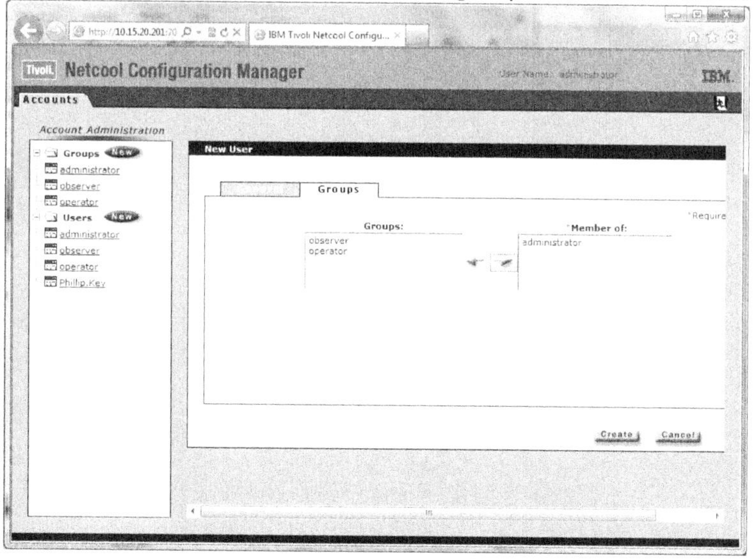

Create a script

From within the ITNCM Web GUI go to New->Native Command Set. This will present the following form:

Once created, right click on the newly created script and select Edit:

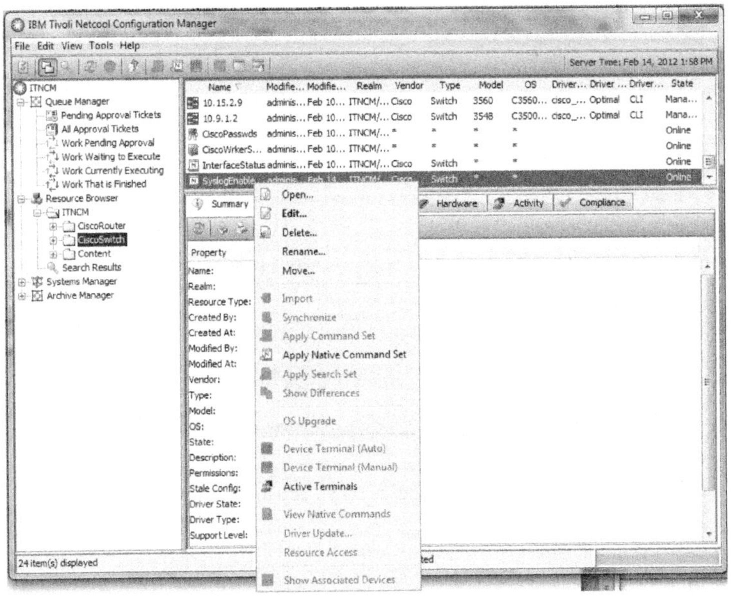

A new window will appear. Select in the Type drop down menu field: Configuration Change and then provide the native commands. (NOTE: "config t" and "end; write mem" are implied at the beginning and end of the script respectively and thus do not need to be included.

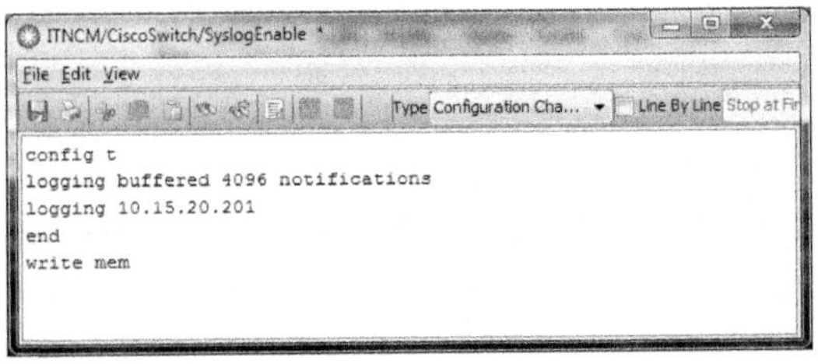

Once complete click File->Save

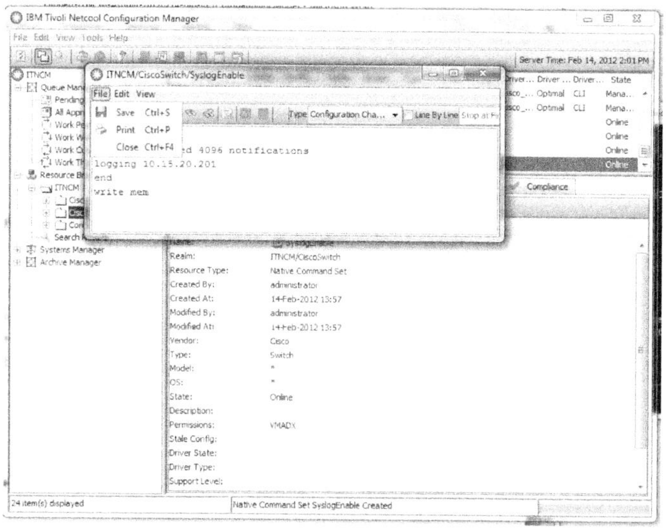

Run a script

The next step is to run the script. This can be done either from the device or from the script. In this case right click on the Script and select Open.

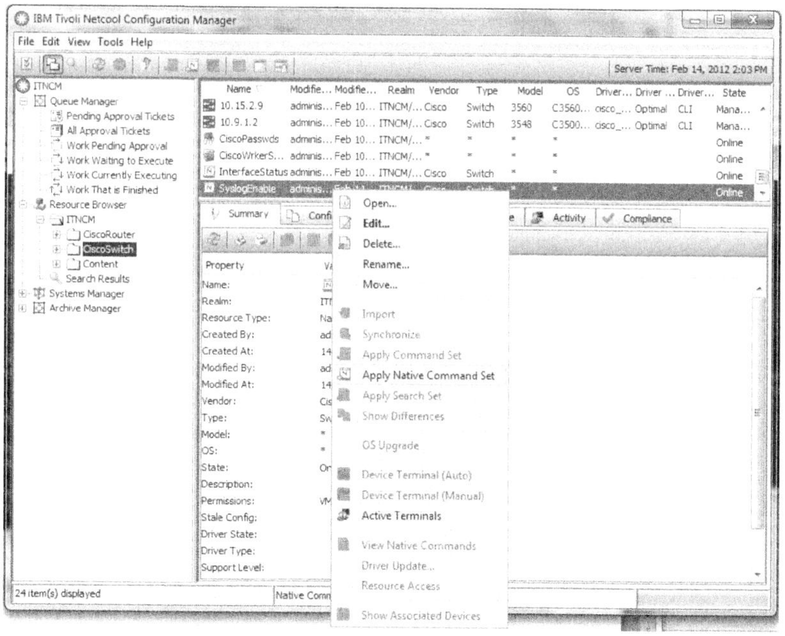

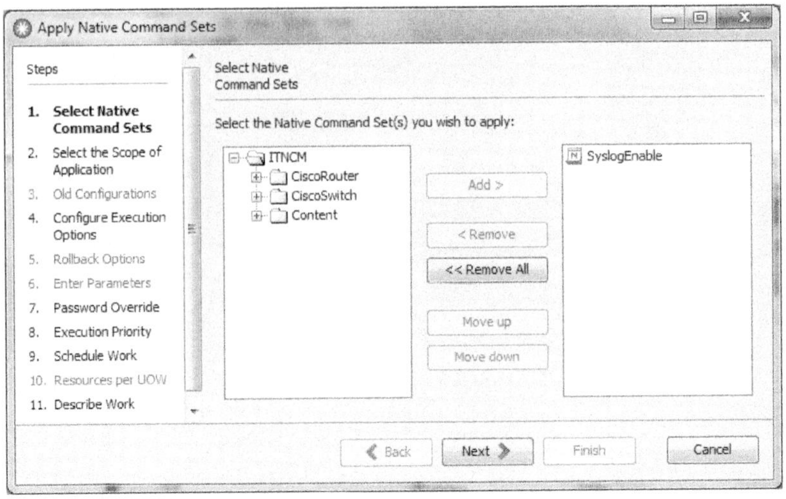
Apply Native Command Sets
Steps
1. Select Native Command Sets
2. Select the Scope of Application
3. Old Configurations
4. Configure Execution Options
5. Rollback Options
6. Enter Parameters
7. Password Override
8. Execution Priority
9. Schedule Work
10. Resources per UOW
11. Describe Work
Select Native Command Sets
Select the Native Command Set(s) you wish to apply:
ITNCM
CiscoRouter
CiscoSwitch
Content
Add >
< Remove
<< Remove All
Move up
Move down
SyslogEnable
Back
Next
Finish
Cancel

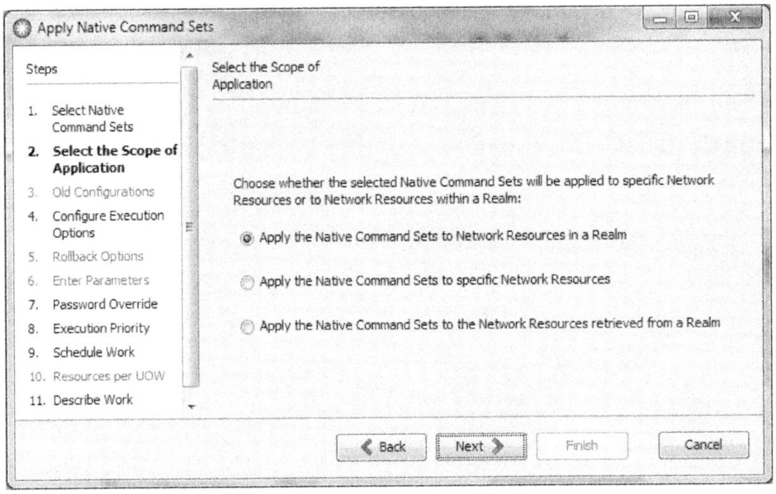
Apply Native Command Sets
Steps
1. Select Native Command Sets
2. Select the Scope of Application
3. Old Configurations
4. Configure Execution Options
5. Rollback Options
6. Enter Parameters
7. Password Override
8. Execution Priority
9. Schedule Work
10. Resources per UOW
11. Describe Work
Select the Scope of Application
Choose whether the selected Native Command Sets will be applied to specific Network Resources or to Network Resources within a Realm:
Apply the Native Command Sets to Network Resources in a Realm
Apply the Native Command Sets to specific Network Resources
Apply the Native Command Sets to the Network Resources retrieved from a Realm
Back
Next
Finish
Cancel

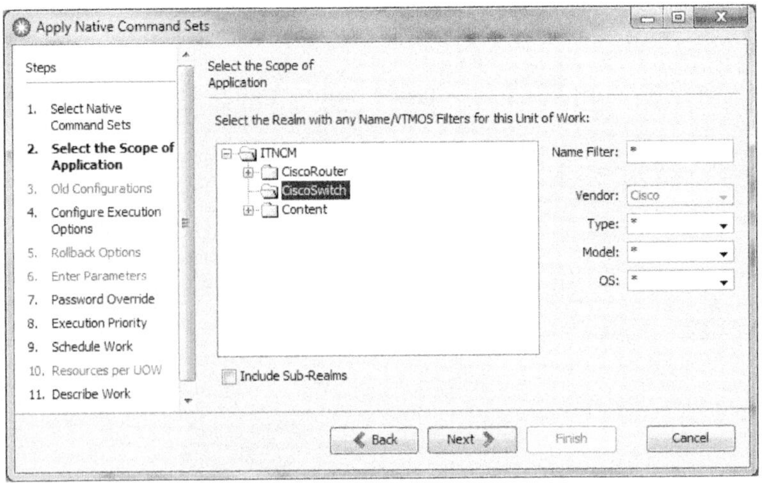
Apply Native Command Sets
Steps
1. Select Native Command Sets
2. Select the Scope of Application
3. Old Configurations
4. Configure Execution Options
5. Rollback Options
6. Enter Parameters
7. Password Override
8. Execution Priority
9. Schedule Work
10. Resources per UOW
11. Describe Work
Select the Scope of Application
Select the Realm with any Name/VTMOS Filters for this Unit of Work:
ITNCM
CiscoRouter
CiscoSwitch
Content
Name Filter: *
Vendor: Cisco
Type: *
Model: *
OS: *
Include Sub-Realms
Back
Next
Finish
Cancel

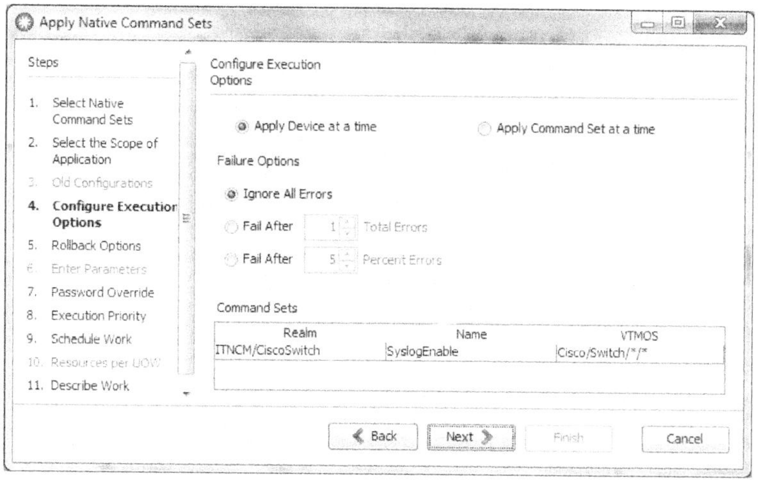
Apply Native Command Sets
Steps
1. Select Native Command Sets
2. Select the Scope of Application
3. Old Configurations
4. Configure Execution Options
5. Rollback Options
6. Enter Parameters
7. Password Override
8. Execution Priority
9. Schedule Work
10. Resources per UOW
11. Describe Work
Configure Execution Options
Apply Device at a time
Apply Command Set at a time
Failure Options
Ignore All Errors
Fail After 1 Total Errors
Fail After 5 Percent Errors
Command Sets
Realm
Name
VTMOS
ITNCM/CiscoSwitch
SyslogEnable
Cisco/Switch/*/*
Back
Next
Finish
Cancel

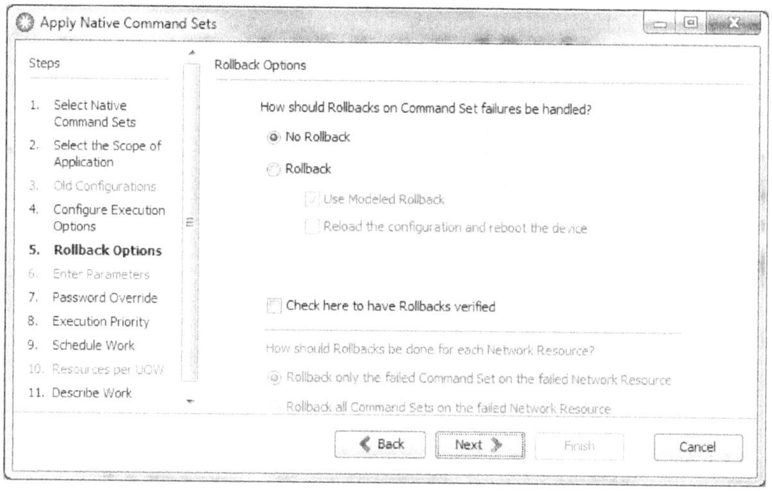
Apply Native Command Sets
Steps
1. Select Native Command Sets
2. Select the Scope of Application
3. Old Configurations
4. Configure Execution Options
5. Rollback Options
6. Enter Parameters
7. Password Override
8. Execution Priority
9. Schedule Work
10. Resources per UOW
11. Describe Work
Rollback Options
How should Rollbacks on Command Set failures be handled?
No Rollback
Rollback
Use Modeled Rollback
Reload the configuration and reboot the device
Check here to have Rollbacks verified
How should Rollbacks be done for each Network Resource?
Rollback only the failed Command Set on the failed Network Resource
Rollback all Command Sets on the failed Network Resource
Back
Next
Finish
Cancel

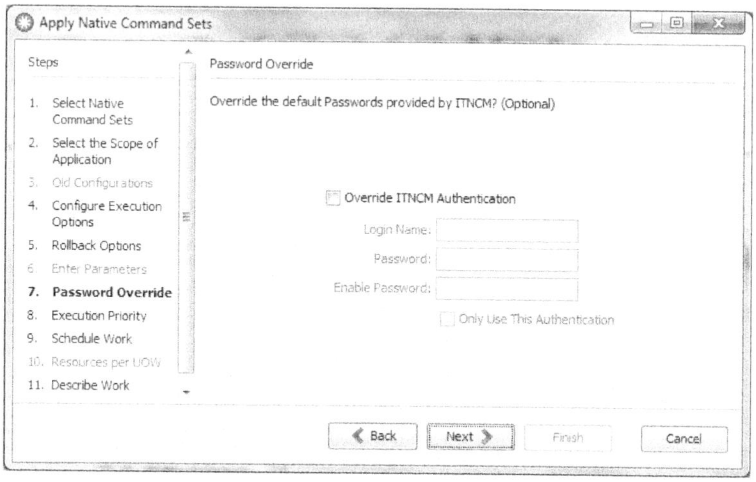
Apply Native Command Sets
Steps
1. Select Native Command Sets
2. Select the Scope of Application
3. Old Configurations
4. Configure Execution Options
5. Rollback Options
6. Enter Parameters
7. Password Override
8. Execution Priority
9. Schedule Work
10. Resources per UOW
11. Describe Work
Password Override
Override the default Passwords provided by ITNCM? (Optional)
Override ITNCM Authentication
Login Name:
Password:
Enable Password:
Only Use This Authentication
Back
Next
Finish
Cancel

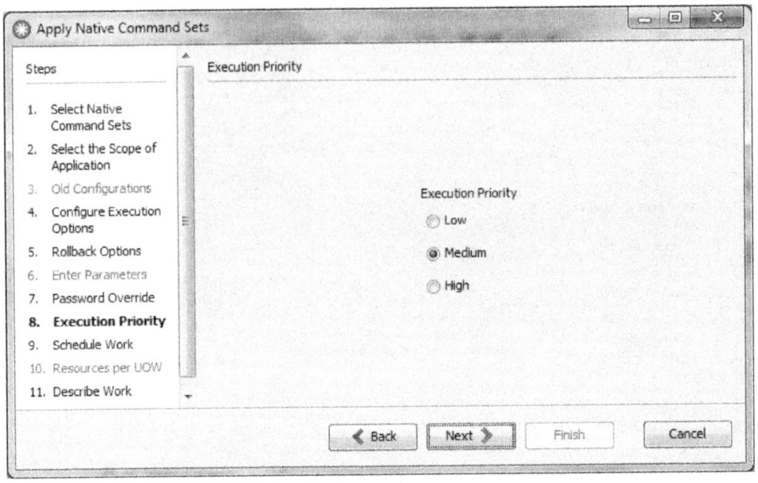
Apply Native Command Sets
Steps
1. Select Native Command Sets
2. Select the Scope of Application
3. Old Configurations
4. Configure Execution Options
5. Rollback Options
6. Enter Parameters
7. Password Override
8. Execution Priority
9. Schedule Work
10. Resources per UOW
11. Describe Work
Execution Priority
Execution Priority
Low
Medium
High
Back
Next
Finish
Cancel

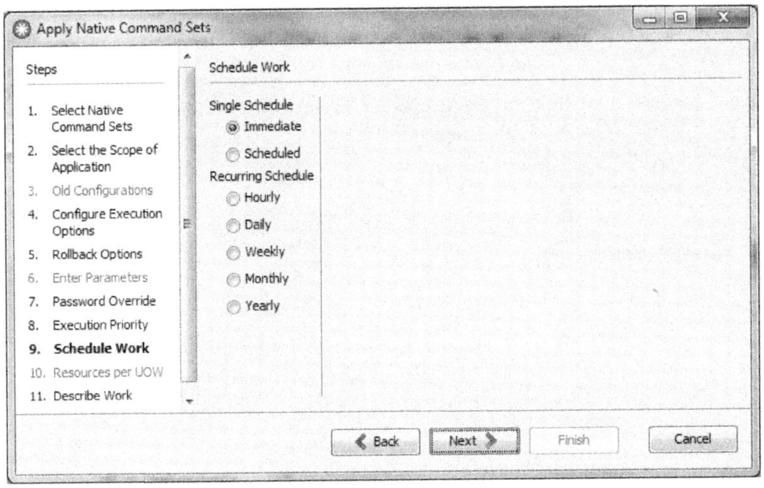
Apply Native Command Sets
Steps
1. Select Native Command Sets
2. Select the Scope of Application
3. Old Configurations
4. Configure Execution Options
5. Rollback Options
6. Enter Parameters
7. Password Override
8. Execution Priority
9. Schedule Work
10. Resources per UOW
11. Describe Work
Schedule Work
Single Schedule
Immediate
Scheduled
Recurring Schedule
Hourly
Daily
Weekly
Monthly
Yearly
Back
Next
Finish
Cancel

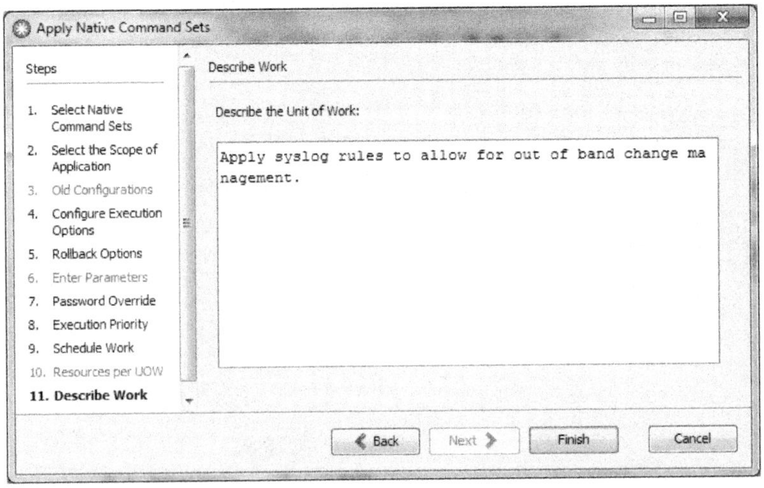
Apply Native Command Sets
Steps
1. Select Native Command Sets
2. Select the Scope of Application
3. Old Configurations
4. Configure Execution Options
5. Rollback Options
6. Enter Parameters
7. Password Override
8. Execution Priority
9. Schedule Work
10. Resources per UOW
11. Describe Work
Describe Work
Describe the Unit of Work:
Apply syslog rules to allow for out of band change ma
nagement.
Back
Next
Finish
Cancel

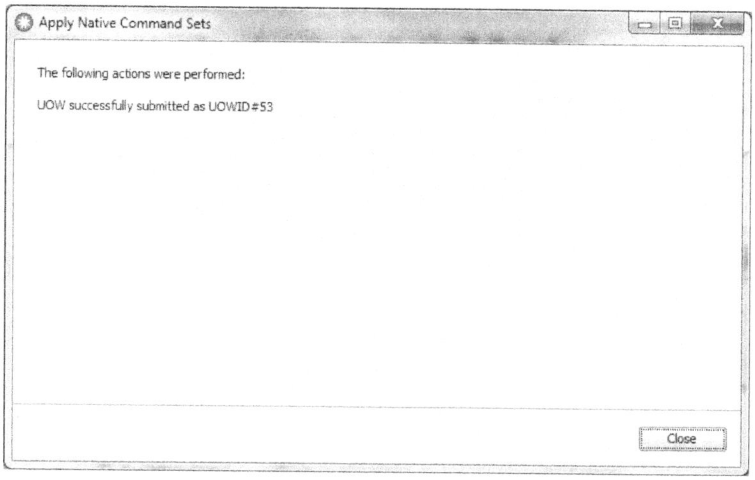

Changing Interactive Pool Size

The number of simultaneous connections to devices and users is determined by the pool size. These are adjusted through the ITNCM Web tool. First login as administrator/administrator and get the following screen

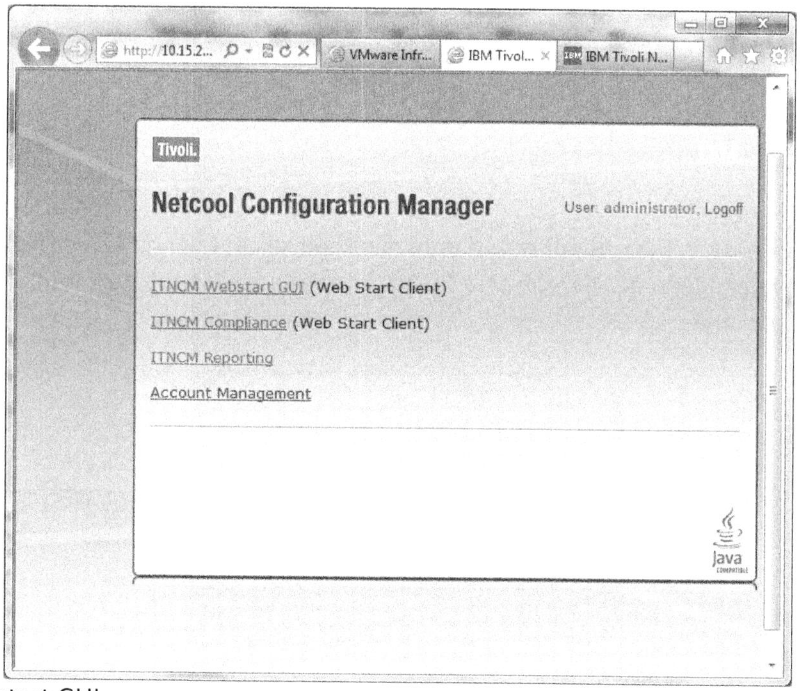

Click ITNCM Webstart GUI

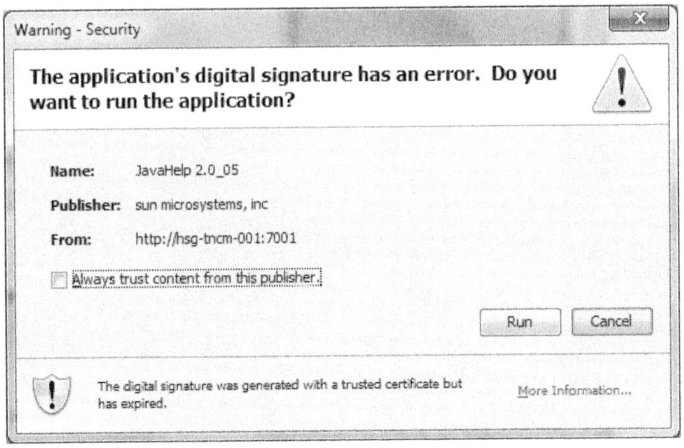

Once the JAVA application is up expand System Manager in the left-hand menu and click on Servers.

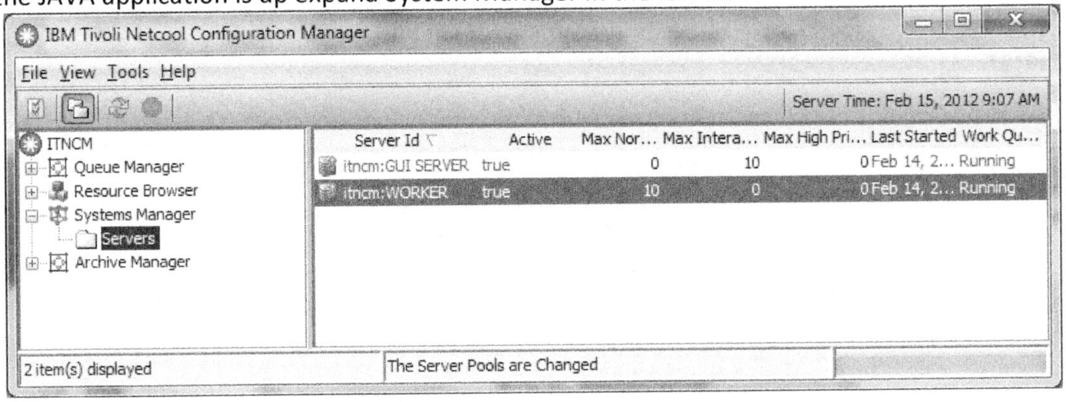

Select the GUI Server in the main window and right click and select Change Server Pool Sizes. The following window will appear. Modify the Max Interactive Pool Size to the maximum number of connections you need and click OK.

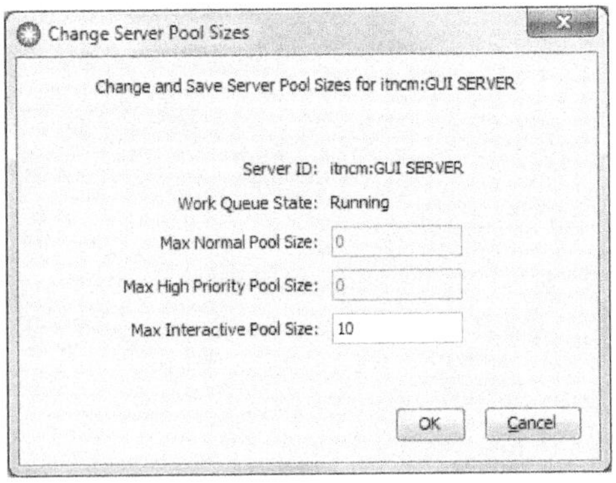

Next, click on the Worker line in the main window and right click and select Change Server Pool Sizes

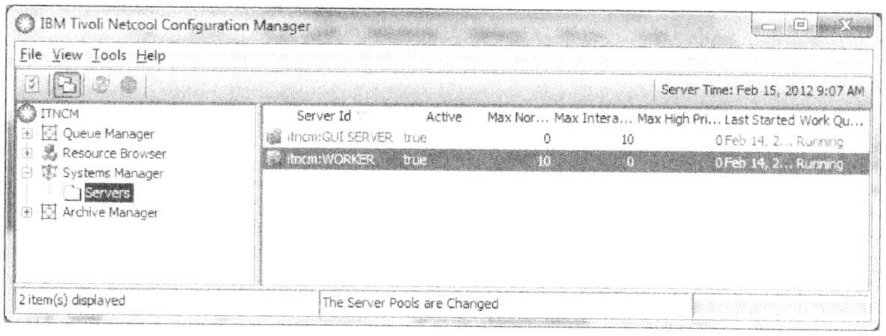

The following window will appear:

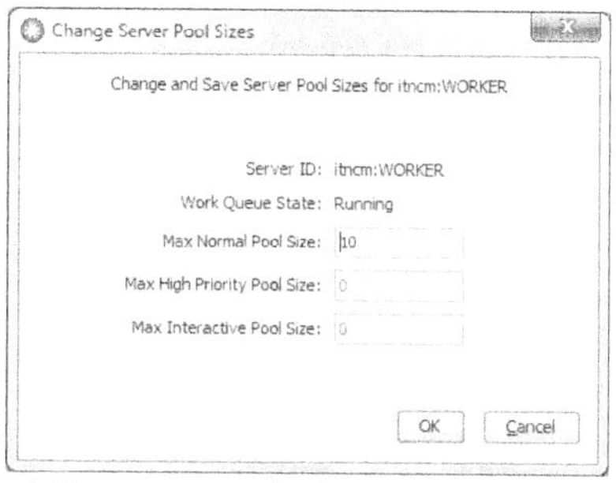

Change the value of Max Normal Pool Size to match the number of simultaneous device threads desired. For example in this case set to 10 the ITNCM server will simultaneously connect to 10 devices when performing scripts.

Validate Housekeeping

Over time ITNCM stores a lot of information about processed configurations. As a result housekeeping is required to keep the database from expanding out of control.

First, validate housekeeping is turned on

```
cd /opt/IBM/tivoli/netcool/ncm/compliance/config/properties
vi WorkFlowManager.properties
```

The last two lines refer to housekeeping:

```
houseKeepingEnabled=true
houseKeepingStartHour=5
```

Create Log Rolling

To set up log compression every 30 days and log deletion every 180 days enter the following:

```
su - icosuser
crontab -e
  i
  30 03 * * * /opt/IBM/tivoli/netcool/ncm/bin/utils/logcleaner.sh 30
      180
  CTRL-[
  ZZ
      crontab: installing new crontab
```

```
crontab -l
30 03 * * * /opt/IBM/tivoli/netcool/ncm/bin/utils/logcleaner.sh 30 180
/opt/IBM/tivoli/netcool/ncm/bin/utils/logcleaner.sh 30 180
# NO ERROR INDICATES THE COMMAND WORKED
```

Summary

ITNCM is a recent acquisition that fills the Configuration Management gap in IBM's Tivoli solution. Placed among the other Netcool products acquired from Micromuse, everything from the approach of ITNCM to the jargon used to the proprietary scripting language employed is completely distinct from the rest of the Netcool suite.

ITNCM - POC Guide provides a "simple" step by step installation guide that walks the reader through a start to finish Proof Of Concept installation of ITNCM.

APPENDIX A: PMR (IBM Trouble Tickets)

Introduction

The common way of resolving any product issues and involving IBM is through opening a PMR. These can be opened online at:
https://www-946.ibm.com/support/servicerequest/prodCompSelect.action?userType=0

PMR 46374,005,000: - Linux /etc/init.d Start and Stop Script not created.

Introduction

46374 005 000 was used to prove out the PMR process. This script is created by following the steps on page 58 in the Installation Guide.

Symptom

Create auto start scripts in /etc/init.d for ITNCM.

Problem

RTFM.

Resolution

RTFM. (The solution is in the ITNCM Installation and Configuration Guide.)

PMR 46380 005 000: - Installation of reports failed as part of Core installation...

Introduction

46380 005 000 was opened when TCR failed to install as part of ITNCM installation.

Symptom

The installation indicated:

```
===================================================================

Install Complete
----------------
```

```
The installation of ITNCM is complete, but some errors occurred during
the install. Please see /opt/IBM/tivoli/netcool/ncm/ITNCM-
Base_InstallLog.log for
details.  Press "Enter" to quit the installer.

When I check the logs I see:
Install Merge Module:     /home/netcool/TNCM-
Install/BASE/NCMReports_linux.iam.zip
                          Status: SUCCESSFUL
                          Additional Notes: NOTE - Installing:
NCMReports_linux.iam.zip

ITNCM-Reports failed to install. Please see the
/opt/IBM/tivoli/netcool/ncm/ITNCMReports_InstallLog.log for further
details.
                          Status: ERROR
                          Additional Notes: ERROR - ITNCM-Reports
failed to install

Custom Action:            com.intelliden.installanywhere.LogErrorAction
                          Status: SUCCESSFUL
```

Problem

TCR Linux requirements are not included in the ITNCM manual. Most of the OS packages were installed but not the openmotif22 package:

Important: Because Tivoli Common Reporting installs 32-bit binaries, you must install the 32-bit versions of the prerequisite libraries, even on 64-bit system. Otherwise, the installation will fail.

```
#Red Hat Enterprise Linux 5.1 32-bit and 64-bit Tolerate
#Restriction: The following system libraries need to be installed:
#yum install compat-libstdc++-33          # -33.3.2.3
#yum install compat-glibc                 #-2.3.4-2.26
yum install openmotif22            #-2.2.3-18
```

Resolution

The package was installed. Also the ITNCM Database user was changed from db2inst1 to icosuser. This was fixed by enabling the regular expression matching for the icosuser as well as db2inst1. (Required changing the database cursor and running the load jar package command. The section in this document was updated to include this change.

```
cd /opt/IBM/tivoli/netcool/ncm/autodiscovery
[icosuser@tncm-001 autodiscovery]$ cat company.txt
a:RtrCredential
p:RtrCredential
e:RtrCredential
d:./results
r:ITNCM/CiscoRtr
10.15.2.14
```

```
10.15.2.3
10.15.2.9
10.15.2.28
10.15.2.23
10.15.2.15
10.15.2.16
10.15.2.6
10.15.2.22
10.15.2.4
10.15.2.8
10.15.2.1
10.15.2.7
10.15.2.5
10.15.2.35
10.15.2.31
10.15.2.32
10.15.2.33
10.9.1.2
[icosuser@tncm-001 autodiscovery]$ ./autodiscover.sh company.txt

Intelliden (c) 2011 - AutoDiscovery Version 6.3.0.0

Started AutoDiscovery Scan At: 13:09:30 - 06/02/2012

------------------------------------------------------------------------
----
Auto Discovery Settings :
Device Info File:  company.txt
        Connection   Type: telnet,ssh,snmpv3
        SSH Port: 22
        Telnet Port: 23,22
        TimeOut: 20
        Custom Rad: false
        Number Of Threads: 10
------------------------------------------------------------------------
----
Attempting Login with the following Account / Password group
               ***** Using Account:  RtrCredential *****
               ***** Using Password: RtrCredential *****
------------------------------------------------------------------------
----
IP Address: 10.15.2.9
  1. Connected to device: telnet
  2. Using port: 23
  3. Logged in: RtrCredential/RtrCredential
  4. Logged into enable mode: RtrCredential
  4. VTMOS determined: Cisco/Switch/3560/12.2(25)SEB1
------------------------------------------------------------------------
----
IP Address: 10.15.2.23
  1. Connected to device: telnet
  2. Using port: 23
  3. Logged in: RtrCredential/RtrCredential
  4. Logged into enable mode: RtrCredential
  4. VTMOS determined: Cisco/Switch/2960/12.2(44)SE
------------------------------------------------------------------------
----
```

```
IP Address: 10.15.2.4
  1. Connected to device: telnet
  2. Using port: 23
  3. Logged in: RtrCredential/RtrCredential
  4. Logged into enable mode: RtrCredential
  4. VTMOS determined: Cisco/Switch/3560/12.2(25)SEB4
-----------------------------------------------------------------------
----
IP Address: 10.15.2.22
  1. Connected to device: telnet
  2. Using port: 23
  3. Logged in: RtrCredential/RtrCredential
  4. Logged into enable mode: RtrCredential
  4. VTMOS determined: Cisco/Switch/2960/12.2(35)SE5
-----------------------------------------------------------------------
----
IP Address: 10.15.2.28
  1. Connected to device: telnet
  2. Using port: 23
  3. Logged in: RtrCredential/RtrCredential
  4. Logged into enable mode: RtrCredential
  4. VTMOS determined: Cisco/Switch/2960/12.2(46)SE
-----------------------------------------------------------------------
----
IP Address: 10.15.2.15
  1. Connected to device: telnet
  2. Using port: 23
  3. Logged in: RtrCredential/RtrCredential
  4. Logged into enable mode: RtrCredential
  4. VTMOS determined: Cisco/Switch/3560/12.2(44)SE
-----------------------------------------------------------------------
----
IP Address: 10.15.2.3
  1. Connected to device: telnet
  2. Using port: 23
  3. Logged in: RtrCredential/RtrCredential
  4. Logged into enable mode: RtrCredential
  4. VTMOS determined: Cisco/Switch/3560/12.2(25)SEE2
-----------------------------------------------------------------------
----
IP Address: 10.15.2.14
  1. Connected to device: telnet
  2. Using port: 23
  3. Logged in: RtrCredential/RtrCredential
  4. Logged into enable mode: RtrCredential
  4. VTMOS undetermined: Cisco/Switch/4506/unknown
-----------------------------------------------------------------------
----
IP Address: 10.15.2.16
  1. Connected to device: telnet
  2. Using port: 23
  3. Logged in: RtrCredential/RtrCredential
  4. Logged into enable mode: RtrCredential
  4. VTMOS determined: Cisco/Switch/3560/12.2(25)SEE3
-----------------------------------------------------------------------
----
IP Address: 10.15.2.1
```

```
  1. Connected to device: telnet
  2. Using port: 23
  3. Logged in: RtrCredential/RtrCredential
  4. Logged into enable mode: RtrCredential
  4. VTMOS determined: Cisco/Switch/3750/12.2(35)SE5
------------------------------------------------------------------------
----
IP Address: 10.15.2.31
  1. Connected to device: telnet
  2. Using port: 23
  3. Logged in: RtrCredential/RtrCredential
  4. Logged into enable mode: RtrCredential
  4. VTMOS determined: Cisco/Switch/2960/12.2(35)SE5
------------------------------------------------------------------------
----
IP Address: 10.15.2.32
  1. Connected to device: telnet
  2. Using port: 23
  3. Logged in: RtrCredential/RtrCredential
  4. Logged into enable mode: RtrCredential
  4. VTMOS determined: Cisco/Switch/2960/12.2(44)SE
------------------------------------------------------------------------
----
IP Address: 10.15.2.8
  1. Connected to device: telnet
  2. Using port: 23
  3. Logged in: RtrCredential/RtrCredential
  4. Logged into enable mode: RtrCredential
  4. VTMOS determined: Cisco/Switch/3550/12.2(25)SEB4
------------------------------------------------------------------------
----
IP Address: 10.9.1.2
  1. Connected to device: telnet
  2. Using port: 23
  3. Logged in: RtrCredential/RtrCredential
  4. Logged into enable mode: RtrCredential
  4. VTMOS determined: Cisco/Switch/3548/12.0(5.3)WC(1)
------------------------------------------------------------------------
----
IP Address: 10.15.2.6
  1. Connected to device: telnet
  2. Using port: 23
  3. Logged in: RtrCredential/RtrCredential
  4. Logged into enable mode: RtrCredential
  4. VTMOS undetermined: Cisco/Switch/2950/unknown
------------------------------------------------------------------------
----
IP Address: 10.15.2.5
  1. Connected to device: telnet
  2. Using port: 23
  3. Logged in: RtrCredential/RtrCredential
  4. Logged into enable mode: RtrCredential
  4. VTMOS undetermined: Cisco/Switch/2950/unknown
------------------------------------------------------------------------
----
IP Address: 10.15.2.7
  1. Connected to device: telnet
```

```
  2. Using port: 23
  3. Logged in: RtrCredential/RtrCredential
  4. Logged into enable mode: RtrCredential
  4. VTMOS undetermined: Cisco/Switch/2950/unknown
-----------------------------------------------------------------------
----
IP Address: 10.15.2.35
  1. Connected to device: telnet
  2. Using port: 23
  3. Logged in: RtrCredential/RtrCredential
  4. Logged into enable mode: RtrCredential
  4. VTMOS undetermined: unknown/unknown/unknown/unknown
-----------------------------------------------------------------------
----


Finished AutoDiscovery Scan At: 13:10:00 - 06/02/2012
  See './results/' for results files

cd results
[icosuser@tncm-001 results]$ pwd
/opt/IBM/tivoli/netcool/ncm/autodiscovery/results
[icosuser@tncm-001 results]$ icosutil BulkLoader -l administrator -p
administrator -f 20120206130930-BulkLoad.csv
-bash: icosutil: command not found
[icosuser@tncm-001 results]$ /opt/IBM/tivoli/netcool/ncm/bin/icosutil
BulkLoader -l administrator -p administrator -f 20120206130930-
BulkLoad.csv
Using local ip: WebGUI-TIP-Server
=======================================
Importing: 10.15.2.9/Cisco/Switch/3560/12.2(25)SEB1 - On line 2
Importing: 10.15.2.23/Cisco/Switch/2960/12.2(44)SE - On line 3
Importing: 10.15.2.4/Cisco/Switch/3560/12.2(25)SEB4 - On line 4
Importing: 10.15.2.22/Cisco/Switch/2960/12.2(35)SE5 - On line 5
Importing: 10.15.2.28/Cisco/Switch/2960/12.2(46)SE - On line 6
Importing: 10.15.2.15/Cisco/Switch/3560/12.2(44)SE - On line 7
Importing: 10.15.2.3/Cisco/Switch/3560/12.2(25)SEE2 - On line 8
Importing: 10.15.2.16/Cisco/Switch/3560/12.2(25)SEE3 - On line 9
Importing: 10.15.2.1/Cisco/Switch/3750/12.2(35)SE5 - On line 10
Importing: 10.15.2.31/Cisco/Switch/2960/12.2(35)SE5 - On line 11
Importing: 10.15.2.32/Cisco/Switch/2960/12.2(44)SE - On line 12
Importing: 10.15.2.8/Cisco/Switch/3550/12.2(25)SEB4 - On line 13
Importing: 10.9.1.2/Cisco/Switch/3548/12.0(5.3)WC(1) - On line 14
```

PMR 46695 005 000: - OOBC and customer connect. ..

Introduction

46695 005 000 was opened to facilitate IBM and Customer interactions going forward after the end of the project. Also some of the OOBC steps were not well documented..

Symptom

OOBC has a few undocumented "features" as part of the installation. This includes automated start and stop as well as the fact that the OOBC user specified in the installation has to be manually created within ITNCM.

Problem

RTFM doesn't work.

Solution

The automated start and stop script in /etc/init.d has to be created. In this case the /etc/init.d/itncm was modified to acconomate the start and stop of OOBC. The actual script is provided in another appendix. Also the OODBuser was created within the ITNCM application. This was documented within this document.

PMR 46560 005 000: - Consolidate Installation Steps

Introduction

46560 005 000 was opened to facilitate the installation of ITNCM and used as a "blank check" to access support to walk through problems. (Also 46559 005 000 was open but closed prematurely.) In particular the installation steps are scattered across three guides: Installation and Configuration, User, and Administration guides. To save time Intelliden support was leaned on to provide "best practices" to the order and approach on the steps.

Symptom

A "normal" installation is poorly documented due to recent changes in the application including the addition of TCR. This ticket was essentially used as a "blank check" for problems encountered in the installation.

Problem

There were three primary areas:

1. Realm, resource access, and device credential creation
2. Group and user creation and setup
3. Very difficult device imports

Solution

The solutions were threefold

1. ITNCM Webstart GUI link: Realm, resource and device credential creation and configuration

2. Account Management: Group and user creation and setup
3. See section on adding a very difficult device.

PMR 46751 005 000: - itncm.sh not recognizing the correct user/passwd

Introduction

46751 005 000 was opened when the normal shutdown process failed though the right Intelliden user and password have been provided.

Symptom

The normal shutdown process fails:

```
su - icosuser
cd /opt/IBM/tivoli/netcool/ncm/bin
./itncm.sh stop
```

This resulted in the following output:

```
IBM Tivoli Netcool Configuration Manager
----------------------------------------

Stopping GUI Server

Please enter the Intelliden Super User and password if prompted below:

Detected Linux RedHat 5
Applying LD_PRELOAD workaround. Ignore any subsequent errors
referencing libfreetype.so
ERROR: ld.so: object '/usr/lib/libfreetype.so.6' from LD_PRELOAD cannot
be preloaded: ignored.
Using /opt/IBM/tivoli/netcool/ncm/tipv2/java/jre/bin/java
ERROR: ld.so: object '/usr/lib/libfreetype.so.6' from LD_PRELOAD cannot
be preloaded: ignored.
ERROR: ld.so: object '/usr/lib/libfreetype.so.6' from LD_PRELOAD cannot
be preloaded: ignored.
ERROR: ld.so: object '/usr/lib/libfreetype.so.6' from LD_PRELOAD cannot
be preloaded: ignored.
ADMU0116I: Tool information is being logged in file

/opt/IBM/tivoli/netcool/ncm/tipv2/profiles/TIPProfile/logs/server1/stop
Server.log
ADMU0128I: Starting tool with the TIPProfile profile
```

```
ADMU3100I: Reading configuration for server: server1
Realm/Cell Name: <default>
Username: Intelliden
Password:
ADMU0111E: Program exiting with error:
javax.management.JMRuntimeException:
           ADMN0022E: Access is denied for the stop operation on Server
MBean
           because of insufficient or empty credentials.
ADMU4113E: Verify that username and password information is correct.
If
           running tool from the command line, pass in the correct -
username
           and -password.  Alternatively, update the
<conntype>.client.props
           file.
ADMU1211I: To obtain a full trace of the failure, use the -trace
option.
ADMU0211I: Error details may be seen in the file:

/opt/IBM/tivoli/netcool/ncm/tipv2/profiles/TIPProfile/logs/server1/stop
Server.log

The Reporting TIP Server is still running.
Please Re-run using the correct TIP Administrator credentials.
```

Problem

The issue disappeared after killing the processes, restarting them normally, and then shutting down the processes normally.

Solution

The issue disappeared after killing the processes, restarting them normally, and then shutting down the processes normally.

APPENDIX B: Rebuilding the schema

The ITNCM schema did not install correctly n the second installation because the ITNCM database user was changed from db2inst1 to icosuser. Once the cursor was changed to the icosuser and the regular expression jar applied to icosuser cursor, then things could execute correctly to allow the creation of the schema. In order to rebuild the schema it was dropped and rebuilt with the following commands:

```
/opt/IBM/tivoli/netcool/ncm/bin/utils/database/dropDBSchema.sh
/opt/IBM/tivoli/netcool/ncm/bin/utils/database/loadDBSchema.sh
```

NOTE: This still resulted in some DB2 errors in the case of the drop schema since some of the objects were not created and resulted in an error when the drop commands were performed:

```
Error: DROP FUNCTION REGEXP_LIKE(VARCHAR(3000),VARCHAR(512),VARCHAR(3))
com.ibm.db2.jcc.am.SqlSyntaxErrorException: DB2 SQL Error: SQLCODE=-
458, SQLSTATE=42883, SQLERRMC=ICOSUSER.REGEXP_LIKE, DRIVER=4.12.55
        at com.ibm.db2.jcc.am.hd.a(hd.java:676)
        at com.ibm.db2.jcc.am.hd.a(hd.java:60)
        at com.ibm.db2.jcc.am.hd.a(hd.java:127)
        at com.ibm.db2.jcc.am.mn.b(mn.java:2290)
        at com.ibm.db2.jcc.am.mn.c(mn.java:2273)
        at com.ibm.db2.jcc.t4.cb.k(cb.java:370)
        at com.ibm.db2.jcc.t4.cb.a(cb.java:62)
        at com.ibm.db2.jcc.t4.q.a(q.java:50)
        at com.ibm.db2.jcc.t4.sb.b(sb.java:220)
        at com.ibm.db2.jcc.am.nn.nc(nn.java:3083)
        at com.ibm.db2.jcc.am.nn.b(nn.java:4037)
        at com.ibm.db2.jcc.am.on.hc(on.java:117)
        at com.ibm.db2.jcc.am.on.execute(on.java:96)
        at
com.ibm.tivoli.ncm.database.SqlScriptLoader.processFile(SqlScriptLoader
.java:347)
        at
com.ibm.tivoli.ncm.database.SqlScriptLoader.executeScriptFiles(SqlScrip
tLoader.java:265)
        at
com.ibm.tivoli.ncm.database.SqlScriptLoader.process(SqlScriptLoader.jav
a:111)
        at
com.ibm.tivoli.ncm.database.SqlScriptLoader.main(SqlScriptLoader.java:9
2)

5 of 8 statement(s) processed successfully.
1 failures due to com.ibm.db2.jcc.am.SqlSyntaxErrorException: DB2 SQL
Error: SQLCODE=-204, SQLSTATE=42704, SQLERRMC=ICOSUSER.DECODE_FUNCTION,
DRIVER=4.12.552 failures due to
com.ibm.db2.jcc.am.SqlSyntaxErrorException: DB2 SQL Error: SQLCODE=-
458, SQLSTATE=42883, SQLERRMC=ICOSUSER.REGEXP_LIKE, DRIVER=4.12.55

Processing file
/opt/IBM/tivoli/netcool/ncm/database/sql/ncm_droptables.sql
```

```
...................................................................
...................................................................
..........
152 of 152 statement(s) processed successfully.
1 failures due to com.ibm.db2.jcc.am.SqlSyntaxErrorException: DB2 SQL
Error: SQLCODE=-204, SQLSTATE=42704, SQLERRMC=ICOSUSER.DECODE_FUNCTION,
DRIVER=4.12.552 failures due to
com.ibm.db2.jcc.am.SqlSyntaxErrorException: DB2 SQL Error: SQLCODE=-
458, SQLSTATE=42883, SQLERRMC=ICOSUSER.REGEXP_LIKE, DRIVER=4.12.55

[icosuser@tncm-001 ~]$
/opt/IBM/tivoli/netcool/ncm/bin/utils/database/loadDBSchema.sh
```

APPENDIX C: DB2/ITNCM/OOBC Start&Stop Commands

Introduction

There are three components to the ITNCM solution that need to be started and stopped:

Component	Description
DB2	DB2 Database
ITNCM	Main ITNCM product
OOBC	Out of Band Control (OOBC) daemon that detects changes to managed network devices that occur outside the product. (i.e. not through either a policy, script, or IDT session.)

DB2

In actuality the DB2 installation adds a daemon watchdog to /etc/inittab - hence why no start or stop script in /etc/init.d. If auto starting was a manual process you could do the following:

```
    su - db2inst1
    db2iauto -on db2inst1
    tail -1 /etc/inittab
  NOTE Output should match:
    fmc:2345:respawn:/opt/ibm/db2/V9.7/bin/db2fmcd #DB2 Fault Monitor
        Coordinator
```

See: http://en.gentoo-wiki.com/wiki/Db2#Starting_and_Stopping_DB2_.28incl._initscript.29

Starting and Stopping DB2 (incl. /etc/init.d script)

DB2 doesn't install an /etc/init.d script for stopping and starting it. Starting and stopping the database instance is done with the following commands, as the database instance owner,

```
su - db2inst1

db2stop

db2start
```

Likewise, the following commands are used to start and stop the administration instance, as the administration instance owner,

```
su - dasusr1

db2admin stop

db2admin start
```

Traditionally, DB2 handles auto-starting at boot time by adding a line to the `/etc/inittab` configuration starting a db2fmcd process, the "DB2 Fault Monitor Coordinator Daemon". This in turn started db2fmd ("DB2 Fault Monitor Daemon") processes, one per database instance configured to auto-start (see below). Each db2fmd process starts it's corresponding database instance, and restarts it in the event of a crash. Likewise, db2fmcd restarts any db2fmd process that crashes, and of course init restarts db2fmcd if it dies. With three layers of auto-restarting processes this is a configuration intended to keep the database running at all costs. However it can be a bit difficult to work with - sometimes it proves insanely difficult to shut down all running DB2 processes (e.g. when installing a fix pack), and of course the procedure of shutting down and restarting things doesn't rely on a nice simple /etc/init.d script - it's all custom DB2 commands.

If you have a production system that absolutely positively must stay running, you should stick with the traditional configuration (if only because IBM support will probably whine at anything abnormal - but then, if you're running Gentoo you're unsupported anyway). On the other hand, if you'd much prefer a nice simple /etc/init.d script and you don't mind handling any crash without the "assistance" of the DB2 Fault Monitor Daemons (although crashes are extremely rare in my experience), then read on:

Firstly, check for and remove (or comment out) any db2fmcd lines at the end of `/etc/inittab`. You may find there's no such line anyway (sometimes the installation doesn't seem to add it although I'm not clear under what circumstances). Next, switch to the database instance owner, and set the instance to auto-start (the /etc/init.d script below only starts instances explicitly set to auto-start, although the stop action tells all DB2 instances to stop, forcibly if necessary, to ensure safe system shutdowns and reboots),

```
su - db2inst1

db2iauto -on db2inst1
```

(The db2iauto command simply sets the DB2AUTOSTART instance-level registry setting to "YES" - you can see this by running `db2set -all` as the database instance owner). Finally, copy the following script into `/etc/init.d/db2` and remember to set its execute bits. Then, if you want DB2 to start and stop along with your other default services,

```
rc-update add db2 default
```

Code: /etc/init.d/db2

```
#!/sbin/runscript

# Path to the DB2 installation
DB2DIR="/opt/ibm/db2/V9.5"

# User name of the administration instance owner
DASUSR=$(${DB2DIR}/instance/daslist)

# List of database instances
DB2INSTS=$(${DB2DIR}/instance/db2ilist)

depend() {
    need net
    use dns clock logger ldap
}

find_homedir() {
    getent passwd $1 | cut -d":" -f 6
}

start() {
    LOGFILE=$(mktemp)
    for db2inst in ${DB2INSTS}; do
        INSTSTART=$(${DB2DIR}/instance/db2iset DB2AUTOSTART -i ${db2inst})
        if [[ ${INSTSTART} == "TRUE" ]] || [[ ${INSTSTART} == "YES" ]]; then
```

```
            ebegin "Starting IBM DB2 database instance ${db2inst}"
            INSTHOME="$(find_homedir ${db2inst})"
            su ${db2inst} -l -c "\
                source ${INSTHOME}/sqllib/db2profile ; \
                db2start" >${LOGFILE} 2>&1
            rc=${?}
            eend ${rc}
            [[ ${rc} -ne 0 ]] && cat ${LOGFILE}
        fi
    done
    if [[ -n "$DASUSR" ]]; then
        ebegin "Starting IBM DB2 administration instance ${DASUSR}"
        INSTHOME="$(find_homedir ${DASUSR})"
        su ${DASUSR} -l -c "\
            source ${INSTHOME}/das/dasprofile ; \
            db2admin start" >${LOGFILE} 2>&1
        rc=${?}
        eend ${rc}
        [[ ${rc} -ne 0 ]] && cat ${LOGFILE}
    fi
    rm -f ${LOGFILE}
}

stop() {
    LOGFILE=$(mktemp)
    if [[ -n "${DASUSR}" ]]; then
        ebegin "Stopping IBM DB2 administration instance ${DASUSR}"
        INSTHOME="$(find_homedir ${DASUSR})"
```

```
        su ${DASUSR} -c "\
            source ${INSTHOME}/das/dasprofile ; \
            db2admin stop" >${LOGFILE} 2>&1
        rc=${?}
        eend ${rc}
        [[ ${rc} -ne 0 ]] && cat ${LOGFILE}
    fi
    for db2inst in ${DB2INSTS}; do
        ebegin "Stopping IBM DB2 database instances ${db2inst}"
        INSTHOME="$(find_homedir ${db2inst})"
        su - ${db2inst} -c "\
            source ${INSTHOME}/sqllib/db2profile ; \
            db2stop force" >${LOGFILE} 2>&1
        rc=${?}
        eend ${rc}
        [[ ${rc} -ne 0 ]] && cat ${LOGFILE}
    done
    rm -f ${LOGFILE}
}
```

ITNCM and OOBC Start and Stop script

Commands were issued to create the ITNCM script which is described in the main document. However, this script had 2 issues. First, it inserted the full path to ITNCM with embedded double quotation marks. This made the various references syntactically incorrect since the paths were already embedded within double quotes. Second, the script failed to allow for the start and stop of the OOBC daemon. The following script was used to replace the defective script:

```
[root@tncm-001 run1]# cat /etc/init.d/itncm
#!/bin/sh

# itncmd       Start IBM Tivoli Netcool Configuration Manager
#
```

```
# chkconfig: 345 99 1
# description: Starts and stops IBM Tivoli Netcool Configuration
Manager software

case "$1" in
'start')
        if [ -f /var/lock/subsys/itncm ]; then
                echo "E:  IBM Tivoli Netcool Configuration Manager
already started"
                exit -1
        fi
        if [ -f /opt/IBM/tivoli/netcool/ncm/bin/itncm.sh ]; then
                su - icosuser -c
"/opt/IBM/tivoli/netcool/ncm/bin/itncm.sh start"
                su - icosuser -c
"/opt/oobc/OutOfBandChange/run1/oobc.sh start"
                touch /var/lock/subsys/itncm
        fi
        ;;

'stop')
        if [ -f /opt/IBM/tivoli/netcool/ncm/bin/itncm.sh ]; then
                su - icosuser -c
"/opt/IBM/tivoli/netcool/ncm/bin/itncm.sh stop"
                su - icosuser -c
"/opt/oobc/OutOfBandChange/run1/oobc.sh stop"
                if [ -f /var/lock/subsys/itncm ]; then
                        rm /var/lock/subsys/itncm
                fi
        fi
        ;;

*)
        echo "IBM Tivoli Netcool Configuration Manager Usage: $0 {
start | stop }"
        exit 1
        ;;
esac
exit 0
```

Also note when you stop ITNCM, it will likely prompt for the username and password of ITNCM (Intelliden/PASSWORD) and also for TIP (TCR) which is tipadmin/PASSWORD.

APPENDIX D: Troubleshooting Device Adds

Like many JAVA based products, ITNCM has bugs here and there, but unlike most JAVA products it is rather stable. The primary Intelliden log can be accessed as follows:

```
su - icosuser
cd /opt/IBM/tivoli/netcool/ncm/logs/
tail -f Intelliden.log
```

The other trick is to turn on the Java Console. In Windows7 this is in Control Panel->Programs->JAVA

Click on the Advanced Tab and expand the Settings: Debugging and Java Console. Turn on all debugging options and select "Show Console"

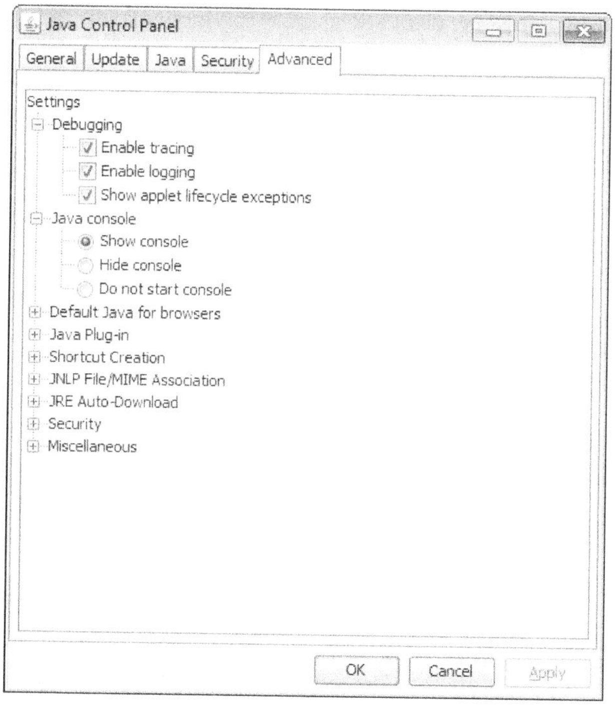

In this case one of the switches was not being imported easily. Using these techniques IBM support could see the program was not operating as expected. The solution was to delete the device and start over using the Adding a "Very Difficult" Device steps in this document.

APPENDIX D: Glossary

Introduction

More than most products, ITNCM has its acronyms. Surprisingly these come not from IBM for the most part but the original Intelliden company. As a result "jargon" can be the greatest barrier to understanding the product. This appendix provides layman's translations of some of the more annoying terms.

Command Set

This basically is a list of commands to run on the managed device. For example a Native Command Set might contain:

```
snmp-server contact $snmp-contact=Russell Crowe$
snmp-server location $snmp-location=Somewhere in Australia$
```

Also Command Sets can be generic and written in ITNCM's own generic language. However, there is a learning curve with this approach.

Command Sets DO NOT specify how ITNCM communicates with the managed devices. This is handled through scripts and resource access widgets.

IDT

In a nutshell this means either a telnet or ssh session to a managed device.

RAD (Resource Access Documentation)

As stated in Chapter 4: Device Communication of the ITNCM Administration Guide, RAD is an XML document that ITNCM base uses to communicate with devices on the Network. The RAD has all the information required to communicate with the device. The RAD controls the device connection for IDT and UOWs. In the case of this POC, no changes are required since telnet, rather than ssh, can be used to access devices.

What RAD does NOT mean anything about the IBM Tivoli Netcool TBSM product. In fact they came from different companies entirely. IBM Tivoli Netcool TBSM originated from Micromuse, while IBM Tivoli Netcool Configuration Manager originated from Intelliden.

Realm

In a nutshell this mean folder. The product is set up to organize managed devices in a hierarchy structure. This same structure is used to divide up the management work among the worker servers. Realm are the structures/folders that allow for hierarchical organization.

What Realm DOES NOT MEAN is IBM's TIP/Websphere use of the term. In particular ITNCM's use of Realm has nothing to do with LDAP, X.500 or user and group management.

Script

This basically is a procedural/expect like program that tells ITNCM now to talk to the device. For example, for Login it may indicate to wait until you see "ame:" and then respond with the user name and then wait for the text "assword:" and then respond with the password for the device. Resource access documents can provide a wrapper around the script and further specify how ITNCM should connect to the device (i.e. telnet verses ssh, etc.)

It does NOT mean an adhoc Command Set to be ran on the devices. Though these are similar the difference is that the Command Set is adhoc and often a Native Command set which is in the language of the managed device such as IOS commands.

VTMOS (Vendor Type, Model, and Operating System)

Vendor Type, Model, and Operating System (VTMOS) is what the auto discovery tool determines in order to categorize the device.

Summary

Hopefully this appendix has shed some light on the confusing terms of ITNCM that often conflict with the other components of Tivoli.

IMPORTANT NOTICE

About NMS Guru

NMS Guru architects and manages comprehensive enterprise management solutions, using Principal Consultants, each with decades of experience and deep roots into the industry. Specialties include: monitoring, performance, configuration, provisioning, change, and security for networks, systems, applications, and business processes. These practices are integrated holistically by weaving together the strategic initiatives from above (OSS/BSS, BPM, ITIL, FCAPS, COBIT, OSS, TMN, etc) with the tactical realities from below (tools, people, knowledge and processes.) The result is increased operational awareness and extended useful lifespan of the enterprise IT management solutions.

NMS Guru is headquartered in Austin, TX (along with IBM Tivoli, CA NetQOS, Spiceworks, SolarWinds, Zenoss, and many others.) For more information, visit our website at http://nmsguru.com or call 1.512.233.1000.

Author

Dan Needles is the founder of NMS Guru. Over the past 20 years as an Enterprise IT Operations Architect, he has created SaaS/ITMaaS solutions as well as designed and implemented Application/System/Network Management and Security solutions and products for over 50 fortune 500 companies and government entities. He can be contacted at guru@nmsguru.com and 1.512.627.6694.

Printed in Dunstable, United Kingdom

91222502R00078